New Wok

To Geraldine and Finn with lots of love and light

New Wok

simple stylish food for the modern cook

SUNIL VIJAYAKAR

WITH PHOTOGRAPHY BY GUS FILGATE

This edition is published by Aquamarine

Aquamarine is an imprint of Anness Publishing Ltd
Hermes House, 88-89 Blackfriars Road, London SE1 8HA
tel. 020 7401 2077; fax 020 7633 9499

www.aquamarinebooks.com; info@anness.com

UK agent: The Manning Partnership Ltd, 6 The Old Dairy,
Melcombe Road, Bath BA2 3LR; tel. 01225 478444;
fax 01225 478440; sales@manning-partnership.co.uk

UK distributor: Grantham Book Services Ltd, Isaac Newton Way,
Alma Park Industrial Estate, Grantham, Lincs NG31 9SD;
tel. 01476 541080; fax 01476 541061; orders@gbs.tbs-ltd.co.uk

North American agent/distributor: National Book Network,
4501 Forbes Boulevard, Suite 200, Lanham, MD 20706;
tel. 301 459 3366; fax 301 429 5746; www.nbnbooks.com

Australian agent/distributor: Pan Macmillan Australia, Level 18,
St Martins Tower, 31 Market St, Sydney, NSW 2000; tel. 1300 135 113;
fax 1300 135 103; customer.service@macmillan.com.au

New Zealand agent/distributor: David Bateman Ltd, 30 Tarndale Grove,
Off Bush Road, Albany, Auckland; tel. (09) 415 7664; fax (09) 415 8892

Publisher Joanna Lorenz
Editorial Director Judith Simons
Senior Editor Susannah Blake
Copy Editors Jane Bamforth and Debbie Foy
Photographer Gus Filgate (with additional images
on pages 12–19 by Nicki Dowey)
Home Economist Sunil Vijayakar
Home Economist's Assistant Emma McIntosh
Stylist Helen Trent
Designer Simon Daley
Jacket Designer Chlöe Steers
Production Controller Steven Lang

10 9 8 7 6 5 4 3 2 1

NOTES

Bracketed terms are intended for American readers.

For all recipes, quantities are given in both metric and imperial measures
and, where appropriate, measures are also given in standard cups and
spoons. Follow one set, but not a mixture, because they are not
interchangeable.

Standard spoon and cup measures are level.

1 tsp = 5ml, 1 tbsp = 15ml, 1 cup = 250ml/8fl oz

Australian standard tablespoons are 20ml. Australian readers should use
3 tsp in place of 1 tbsp for measuring small quantities of gelatine, flour,
salt, etc.

Medium (US large) eggs are used unless otherwise stated.

Contents

From old wok to new wok

Concave in shape with deep sides and a rounded bottom, the wok is one of the oldest and most versatile cooking vessels ever designed. It is thought to have originated in China during the Han Dynasty almost 2000 years ago, and from there its popularity soon spread to other countries in Asia where variations of the original wok are still used today. In Japan there is the wok-shaped tempura pan, in Thailand the *kata*, and in India the *karahi*.

The wok's amazing versatility and natural affinity to quick cooking make it perfect for today's cook who wants fabulous food, but doesn't have time to spend hours slaving in the kitchen. With its high sides and large surface area, the wok is ideal for stir-frying, but is equally well-suited to deep-frying, steaming and simmering. With the array of ingredients available today, the dishes you can whip up in a wok are virtually endless.

Improved availability of exotic ingredients and a growing knowledge of world cuisines has opened up a new dimension to the modern cook, who can bring together the flavours and cooking styles of East and West. The recipes in this book take their influence from Chinese, Indonesian, Thai, Malaysian, Vietnamese, Japanese and Indian cooking, but they also draw on Western traditions to create a fabulous fusion of flavours.

From bitesize snacks and simmered soups to steamed and stir-fried feasts and sweet and sticky desserts – this book offers a wonderful choice of dishes. Using good-quality ingredients, subtle flavourings and simple cooking methods, each dish is absolutely delicious and perfect for any occasion – whether you want to make an informal snack to serve with drinks, a midweek supper, or an elegant dinner to impress family and friends.

Choosing a wok

Traditionally, woks were made from heavy cast iron, but today they are more commonly made from thin carbon steel, which conducts heat quickly and evenly. They must be seasoned before use. Non-stick woks are also widely available and are good for cooking acidic food such as fruit, which will discolour in a steel wok.

Classic woks have a round base and either one long handle or two smaller ones. Single-handled woks are great for stir-frying, while two-handled ones are more stable and are perfect for deep-frying, steaming and braising.

For general use, choose a wok that is 30–35cm/12–14in in diameter, with a domed lid. This is versatile and can be used for most cooking functions.

◄ Woks come in many different shapes and sizes and are good for everyday use.

Seasoning the wok

All new woks, except non-stick ones, need to be seasoned before first use. Scrub the wok in warm, soapy water and place it over a low heat to dry. Add a little cooking oil and, using crumpled kitchen paper, wipe around the pan to coat evenly in the oil. Heat gently for 10–12 minutes, then wipe clean with kitchen paper; the paper will become black. Repeat this process several times until the paper comes away clean and the wok has darkened.

Once seasoned, the wok should never be washed with soap; only use warm or hot water and wipe dry after use. Place the clean wok over a low heat for a few minutes to ensure it is completely dry and to prevent rust forming. (If rust forms, scrub the wok with wire wool, then re-season.) With continued use, the wok will develop its own non-stick coating.

▼ A new carbon steel wok should be seasoned before the first use.

▲ Wire skimmers, slotted spoons, tongs and wooden spatulas are all invaluable utensils for wok cooking.

Wok accessories

Wok lid A well-fitting domed lid prevents evaporation during cooking, particularly when simmering, and is essential for steaming.

Charn This metal, spade-like spatula is essential for stir-frying and is perfectly suited to the scooping, turning action used when stir-frying. It has a long wooden handle making it safe and easy to use over a hot wok.

Chopsticks Long wooden chopsticks can be used for turning fried foods, but long-handled tongs are just as good.

Wire skimmers Available in different sizes, these wire-mesh scoops on long wooden handles are good for safely adding food to, and removing food from, hot oil when deep-frying.

Bamboo steamers Available as single- or multi-tiered baskets of varying sizes, these can be used for steaming bite-size morsels or whole fish or birds.

Trivet Essential for steaming, a folding wooden trivet, or steaming rack, sits in the base of the wok and supports the steamer or plate just above the level of the simmering water.

Tempura racks These curved racks clip on to the wok and can be used for draining deep-fried food and keeping it warm when cooking in batches.

Wok brush This short, stiff brush is used for cleaning steel woks because it does not ruin the seasoned surface.

Wok stand This metal stand should be used when a round-based wok is used on a flat-topped electric stove. It is essential for safe deep-frying.

▼ Traditional bamboo steaming baskets come in many different sizes.

Classic cooking techniques

Stir-frying

This quick, healthy cooking method is one of the most popular wok cooking techniques. Bitesize pieces of food are tossed over a high heat, searing the outside. Only a small quantity of oil is used and the ingredients retain all of their colour, flavour and goodness.

The wide, conical shape of the wok is perfectly suited to this technique. The sides of the pan heat up quickly, providing a large surface area on which to cook the food.

Preparing ingredients Prepare all the ingredients before you start. Wash, peel, chop and slice as necessary and place the ingredients in individual piles so that you can add them to the wok in the right order.

Cut firm vegetables such as carrots, (bell) peppers and courgettes (zucchini) into thin strips or pieces. Cut leafy green vegetables such as Chinese leaves (Chinese cabbage), pak choi (bok choy) and broccoli diagonally to increase their exposed surface area

and decrease their cooking time. Bite-size vegetables such as beansprouts and baby corn can be left whole.

Cut meat, poultry and fish into thin slices, across the grain to help even, quick cooking. Cutting across the grain will also prevent the meat, poultry or fish from disintegrating during cooking. Small shellfish such as prawns (shrimp) can be left whole.

Choosing the right oil Use a bland oil that will not compete with the flavours of the other ingredients. Sunflower and vegetable oils are all perfect for stir-frying. (Strong-tasting oils such as sesame oil should only be used as a flavouring.)

Perfect results Before you start, make sure the wok is clean and dry. Place it over a high heat and, once hot, add the oil and swirl it around the wok to coat the surface. If using aromatics such as onion, garlic, fresh root ginger and chillies, add these first to flavour the oil. Toss over the high heat for 1 minute, then start adding the other

▲ From left to right: Prepare all the ingredients before you start, add them to the wok in order of cooking time, then toss in the flavourings just before serving.

ingredients in order of cooking time. Make sure you keep the food moving continuously, using a tossing action.

Food that requires the longest cooking time, such as meat or poultry, should be added first. Next add firm vegetables such as carrots, peppers and mushrooms and toss for a few minutes before adding tender leafy greens, beans, and beansprouts, which require very brief cooking. Just before serving, toss in flavouring ingredients such as sesame or chilli oils, soy sauce, and chopped fresh herbs.

Stir-fry tips
• When stir-frying large quantities, do it in batches to avoid "stewing" the food.
• Maintain the high temperature of the wok to ensure the food is sealed, trapping all the juices inside.
• Drain marinated food thoroughly before adding it to the wok.

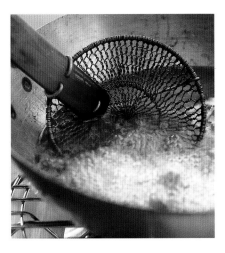

Deep-frying

Submerging food in hot oil produces tasty snacks with a crisp, golden outer layer and a succulent, juicy centre. The wok is the perfect vessel for deep-frying because its concave shape and sloping sides provide a wide surface area for cooking, but it requires less oil than a straight-sided pan. The sloping sides conduct heat well, heating the oil quickly and evenly.

Batters and other coatings Deep-frying cooks food using a very intense heat, and delicate foods such as prawns (shrimp) need to be protected to avoid spoiling their wonderful taste and texture. The most common coatings are either batter, or a layer of cornflour (cornstarch), beaten egg and breadcrumbs or seasoned flour. These ensure that the food becomes crisp and golden on the outside, while remaining moist and tender on the inside. Starchy foods such as potatoes or noodles are more robust and can be fried without a coating.

Choosing the right oil Oils with a mild flavour and low smoking point such as sunflower and vegetable oils are good for deep-frying. Olive oil, sesame oil, butter and margarine are all unsuitable.

Crisp and golden For perfect results, the oil must be heated to the right temperature, so it is worth investing in a cook's thermometer. The temperature may vary depending on the type of food being cooked, so always follow the recipe. If the oil is too hot, the food will burn on the outside before it is cooked inside; if the oil is not hot enough, the food will absorb the oil and become soggy and greasy.

It is best to deep-fry in batches because the oil temperature will drop when food is added. Gently lower the food into the oil, a few pieces at a time, and cook until golden. Lift out using a slotted spoon, drain on kitchen paper and keep warm while you cook the remaining batches. Keep an eye on the temperature of the oil and allow it to return to the correct temperature before adding more food.

▲ From left to right: Protect delicate foods with a wonton wrapper or layer of batter, then deep-fry until golden.

Safety in the kitchen The most important thing to remember when deep-frying is safety.

• Always have a fire blanket or damp dishtowel to hand. If the oil in the wok catches fire, quickly lay the fire blanket or dishtowel over the wok to douse the flames. **Never** throw water on to burning oil – it is very dangerous.

• Make sure that the wok is stable, and use a wok stand if necessary.

• Never fill the wok more than one-third full of oil.

• To prevent hot oil spitting when you add food, bring the food to room temperature and drain off any excess batter or marinade before carefully sliding it into the oil.

• Remove deep-fried food from the hot oil with care, using a slotted spoon, and drain well on kitchen paper.

• Avoid reusing oil for deep-frying. Leave it to cool completely before pouring it into a bottle and discarding.

Steaming

This classic technique uses a moist heat that helps to retain the flavour, texture and goodness of the food. It gives a light, delicate result and offers a perfect contrast to richer, heavier deep-fried and braised dishes.

The narrow base of the wok is ideal for supporting the trivet or steaming rack, while the broad, sloping sides provide a wide surface area of water to produce steam. A two-handled wok is a good choice because it is very stable, but a single-handled wok will be fine.

How to steam There are several ways to steam food in a wok – either on a heatproof plate or in a bamboo or metal steamer. Bamboo steamers come in many sizes and can be stacked up to form a single multi-tiered basket.

Place a trivet or steaming rack in the base of the wok and pour in cold water to reach the level of the trivet or rack. Balance the plate or steamer on top, ensuring it does not touch the water. Cover the wok with a domed lid or, if using a bamboo steamer, simply cover the steamer with the woven bamboo lid. Bring the water to the boil, then reduce the heat and simmer gently until the food is cooked.

Preparing a bamboo steamer Before using a bamboo steamer for the first time, soak it in water for a couple of hours. To steam, line the basket with greaseproof (waxed) paper or banana leaves to prevent food from sticking to the base and pieces of food falling through the slats. You can use scented leaves such as pandanus leaves or kaffir lime leaves to add extra flavour.

Steaming tips Steaming is one of the simplest wok techniques and gives delicious results. Follow these tips to ensure success every time.

• If you are using two or more layers of bamboo steaming baskets, change their positions halfway through, moving the top baskets to the bottom, to ensure the food is evenly cooked.

• If steaming food for longer than 10 minutes, check the water level regularly, adding more if necessary.

• Keep the water at a medium simmer, rather than a rolling boil.

• Steam is very hot and can cause burns, so take care when removing the lid from the wok or steamer.

▲ Banana leaves make the perfect lining for a bamboo steamer. Place a whole red snapper on top, then add aromatics to flavour the fish while it steams.

◄ Dim sum are delicious when steamed: piping hot and wonderfully succulent.

Simmering

As well as frying and steaming, the wok is also perfect for simmering – whether it's blanching vegetables, boiling noodles, simmering soups and stews, or poaching fruit. The versatile shape of the wok allows it to double as a pan and a frying pan, which is essential when making many braised dishes.

Blanching and boiling The wok is perfect for briefly blanching vegetables such as broccoli and carrots, and also for boiling ingredients such as noodles that require a short cooking time. Ensure the wok is stable, using a wok stand if necessary, then fill no more than two-thirds full of water. Bring to a rolling boil, then carefully lower the ingredients into the water and cook for the required length of time. Lift the food out of the wok, using a wire skimmer, and drain well. If blanching precedes a further cooking technique, such as stir-frying, plunge the blanched vegetables into cold water to arrest the cooking process.

Braising Dishes such as soups, stews and curries usually start with frying before adding the cooking liquid and simmering gently until cooked. Before you start, ensure the wok is stable, then stir-fry spices such as cumin and coriander and aromatics such as onion, garlic and fresh root ginger. Add meat, poultry, lentils or vegetables such as potatoes that require lengthy cooking and fry briefly before adding the cooking liquid such as stock or coconut milk. Bring to the boil, then reduce the heat and simmer gently. Stir from time to time to prevent food from sticking to the base of the wok.

The shape of the wok encourages quick evaporation in simmered dishes, so stir regularly and add more liquid if necessary. "Dry" curries and stews are usually cooked without a lid to facilitate evaporation, but dishes with a liquid base such as soups should usually be covered during cooking.

▲ Asian greens such as pak choi are delicious blanched in boiling water and served as an accompaniment to rich Asian-style dishes.

◄ Creamy coconut milk is a popular cooking liquid in many Asian stews and curries. Slow, gentle simmering produces a rich, creamy taste and texture.

◄ Lentils can be simmered with spices and aromatics to make a delicious dhal.

Simmering tips
• Carbon steel woks are not suitable for making really slow, long-simmered dishes because the seasoned layer on the surface of the wok may be stripped away during cooking. Use a non-stick or stainless steel wok instead.
• Woks conduct heat very well, so always cook slow-simmered dishes on as low a heat as possible.
• When cooking noodle soups, be sure to cook the noodles before adding them to the broth. If the noodles are cooked in the soup, they will release starch and make the soup cloudy.

Glossary of ingredients

The recipes in this book make use of many wonderful ingredients from around the world – from fresh herbs, pungent spices and exotic vegetables to aromatic sauces and pastes. Most of the ingredients are available in large supermarkets, while the more unusual ones can be found in Chinese and Asian stores. The list below offers a guide to the ingredients used.

The store-cupboard

The Asian store-cupboard (pantry) contains a wide array of dry and canned ingredients. Some, such as rice and noodles, are everyday staples, while others, such as dried lotus leaves, are less commonly used.

Basmati rice This aromatic, long-grain white rice has a delicious fluffy texture. When cooked, the grains remain firm and separate. Basmati rice is usually served as an accompaniment to wet or dry curry dishes.

▼ Bean thread noodles

▲ Rice paper wrappers

Jasmine rice Also known as fragrant rice, this medium-grain white rice is widely used in Thai and South-east Asian cooking. The grains become slightly sticky when cooked and make an excellent accompaniment.

Egg noodles *See* fresh ingredients.

Bean thread noodles Also known as cellophane or glass noodles, these thin, translucent noodles are made from mung bean and tapioca starch. They are very tough and usually need to be cut with a pair of scissors or soaked in water until supple, then cut into shorter lengths. To prepare, soak them in hot water for 3–4 minutes, or deep-fry until crisp.

Rice vermicelli These thin, translucent noodles are made from rice flour dough and are often used in stir-fries and soups. To prepare, soak in hot water for 8–10 minutes until tender, or deep-fry until crisp.

Rice stick noodles These short, flat, opaque noodles are broader and thicker than rice vermicelli and are also used in stir-fries and soups. To prepare, soak in hot water for 15–20 minutes.

Rice paper wrappers Also known as *bahn trang*, these translucent, paper-thin rounds are used to make spring rolls. The wrappers are made from a rice flour, salt and water dough and left to dry on bamboo mats. They come in different sizes and are available in Asian stores in sealed plastic packets. Soak the wrappers very briefly in a little lukewarm water before wrapping around food and either serving fresh or deep-frying. Take care when handling the dry wrappers because they break easily.

Tofu sheets Usually found in Asian supermarkets, these thin, brittle, pale yellow sheets are made from the dried skin that forms on the surface of boiled soya milk. Soak briefly in water to make them pliable, then wrap around food and steam or deep-fry. Take care when handling because they break easily.

Dried lotus leaves Available in Asian supermarkets, these are the dried leaves of the water lily. The leaves are large, strong and robust, making them perfect for wrapping foods that require longer cooking times. They impart a distinct aroma and flavour to the food enclosed. Soak in warm water for about 35–40 minutes before using and always place the filling on the shiny side of the leaf. (Do not eat the leaf once cooked.)

Nori These very dark green, paper-thin sheets of marine algae are widely used in Japanese cooking. The sheets are most commonly used to wrap food, in particular rice sushi. They may also be snipped into rice salads as a garnish.

Bamboo shoots These pale shoots come from edible varieties of the bamboo plant, which are picked as soon as they appear above ground. They have a crisp yet tender texture and mild flavour. They are widely used in Chinese cooking and are available in cans – either whole or sliced. Drain and rinse well before use.

Water chestnuts This crunchy, white vegetable is widely used in Asian cooking and gives a distinctive texture to many dishes. Although they are occasionally available fresh, still with their purplish skin, they are more usually sold peeled in cans. The canned chestnuts must be drained, rinsed and chopped before cooking.

▼ Fresh water chestnuts

▲ Sesame seeds

Coconut cream and milk Also known as thick coconut milk, coconut cream is extracted from the flesh of fresh coconuts. It has a very thick, creamy consistency and is very rich. Coconut milk has a thinner consistency and is extracted from the coconut flesh, after the cream has been pressed out. They are both widely used in Asian curries, desserts and sweet dishes.

Ghee Also known as clarified butter or pure butter fat, ghee gives a rich, buttery taste to food. It is used widely in Indian cooking, particularly as a flavouring for special rice dishes. It is usually sold in cans and can be found in Asian stores. A mixture of butter and a bland oil can be used instead.

Rice flour This fine powder is made from ground white rice and is available in different grades: fine, medium and thick. It is used in noodles, pastries, batters and coatings, and as a binding and thickening agent.

Besan Also known as gram or chickpea flour, this fine, pale yellow flour is made from ground chickpeas. It is widely used in Indian cooking as an ingredient in batters, and also as a thickening agent in some vegetable dishes.

Sesame seeds Widely used in Asian vegetable dishes, sauces, breads and cookies, these tiny pear-shaped seeds, measuring no more than 3mm/⅛in in length, may be yellow, brown or black. They have a mild, nutty flavour, which can be developed further by roasting.

Desiccated (dry unsweetened shredded) coconut These dried flakes of roughly grated coconut are used widely throughout Asia. Available in most supermarkets, they can be found in sweetened and unsweetened varieties. The sweetened variety is usually used in desserts and baking, while the unsweetened variety is used in savoury dishes and curries, or for coating deep-fried foods.

▼ Ghee

▲ Bird's eye chillies

Fresh ingredients

With improved transport, there is an ever-increasing choice of good-quality, fresh exotic produce available. You should be able to find the ingredients listed here in most large supermarkets or Chinese and Asian stores.

Chillies There are many different types of chilli used in Asian cooking. They form the basis of curry pastes and are used widely as a piquant seasoning. Take care when handling because they can irritate skin and eyes. Always wash your hands with soap and water immediately after handling chillies.
• Bird's eye chillies are small (1–3cm/½–1¼in long) but extremely hot.
• Medium–large chillies (10–20cm/4–8in long) are reasonably hot.

Garlic This aromatic bulb is an integral flavouring in much Asian cooking. It is the most potent member of the onion family and can be used in a wide variety of dishes, from salads and stir-fries to soups and curries. Remove the thin, papery skin of the cloves before crushing, slicing or chopping.

Fresh root ginger This spicy, aromatic root plays a key role in Asian cooking. The light brown, knobbly root has a thin skin that should be removed and discarded before finely chopping, slicing or grating the flesh.

Galangal Similar in appearance to fresh root ginger, galangal is pinkish in colour. It has a distinctive peppery flavour and is used as a spice base for curries. Take care when handling it because the juice stains. Galangal can also be bought in dried powder form, known as Laos powder.

Lemon grass This long, woody herb has a sour-lemon flavour and aroma. To use, trim the base, remove the tough outer leaves and finely slice or chop the white interior. The whole stem can be added to flavour curries and soups; it should be bruised with the back of a knife to release its aroma.

Kaffir lime leaves These perfumed, citrusy, dark green leaves are usually joined together in a figure of eight. Snip finely with a pair of scissors before adding to curries, soups and salads.

▼ Kaffir lime leaves

▲ Chinese chives

Coriander (cilantro) Sometimes known as Chinese parsley, all parts of this aromatic plant are used in Asian cooking. The fresh green leaves have a peppery, earthy flavour and are usually added at the last minute or used as a garnish. The stems and roots are ground and used in curry pastes. The seeds may be used whole or ground to flavour curries and soups. Fresh coriander (cilantro) should be stored in the refrigerator; stand the herb in a glass of water and tie a plastic bag over the top.

Basil There are two varieties of basil used in Asian cooking. Thai, or sweet, basil has slightly serrated leaves and a sweet anise flavour, and is used in stir-fries, red and green curries and salads. Purple, or holy, basil has narrow, dark purple-tinged leaves with a strong clove-like taste and is added to stir-fries and stronger flavoured curries.

Chinese chives Also known as garlic chives, these long, thin, garlic-scented leaves are stronger than the slender Western variety. The edible yellow-white buds make a pretty garnish.

Curry leaves These small, dark green, shiny leaves have a wonderfully spicy fragrance and are used to flavour curries and lentil dishes in southern India, Malaysia and Sri Lanka. They need to be fried in oil to release their flavour. Curry leaves are sold fresh in Asian stores, and they freeze well.

Pak choi (bok choy) Also known as Chinese chard, this member of the cabbage family has white, fleshy stems and green leaves. The whole vegetable can be used – thickly sliced in soups and stir-fries, or sliced lengthways and steamed gently until tender.

Choi sum Also known as Chinese flowering cabbage, choi sum has long, smooth green leaves with pale green stems and pale yellow flowers at the tips of the inner shoots. Slightly bitter with a mustard-leaf flavour, choi sum is good in stir-fries and cooks quickly.

Gai larn Also known as Chinese broccoli, this vegetable has thick green stalks and leathery green leaves with white flowers. It is delicious steamed whole, or thickly sliced and stir-fried.

▼ Pak choi

▲ Fresh egg noodles

Okra These green, ridged pods have a distinctive taste and texture. Choose firm, bright green okra with no signs of browning. It is delicious stir-fried, or added to curries or braised dishes.

Pea aubergines (eggplant) These small, pale green, round aubergines resemble peas. They are firm with a distinctive, slightly bitter taste, and are often used in Thai green curry. You can use a diced large aubergine instead.

Mushrooms Several mushroom varieties are popular in Asian cooking.
• Shiitake mushrooms have dark brown caps, a rich, smoky flavour and meaty texture and are grown on the bark of a particular type of oak tree. They are available fresh and dried.
• Oyster mushrooms are shaped like an oyster shell and are usually pale yellow, grey or brown in colour. More delicate in flavour and texture than the shiitake, they are used in a variety of dishes.
• Enokitake, or enoki, mushrooms grow in clumps. They have tiny white caps and long, thin stalks. They need very little cooking and are added to soups and other dishes at the last minute.

Pandanus leaves These long, green leaves impart a lovely floral aroma to food and are used as a flavouring in Thai and Asian cooking. They should not be eaten, so remove and discard before eating. They can be found in the chilled sections of Asian stores.

Red shallots Also known as Thai shallots, these small pinkish onions are more pungent than brown shallots. They have an intense flavour and are used to flavour savoury dishes, or fried to make a crisp garnish.

Egg noodles Made from wheat and eggs, these yellow noodles are available in a variety of widths. They can be found in the chilled section of Asian stores and will keep for about a week in the refrigerator.

Rice noodles These thick, white noodles need only to be soaked in boiling water before eating or adding to other dishes. They can be found in the chilled section of Asian stores.

Wonton wrappers These thin square sheets are usually made from an egg and wheat flour dough. They are most commonly used to make dumplings or wontons, and are then steamed or deep-fried. They can be found in the chilled section of Asian stores.

Tofu Also known as beancurd, tofu is made from fermented yellow soya beans and pressed into blocks. There are several different varieties. Silken tofu has a smooth texture and is usually added to soups; it is not suitable for stir-frying because it tends to break up. Firm tofu is soft and tender and is suitable for steaming and frying.

Spices and flavourings

As well as fresh herbs and aromatics, the Asian kitchen makes good use of a wide selection of other flavourings – from aromatic spices to pungent sauces and condiments.

Coriander These small, round, light brown seeds have a fragrant flavour and are available whole or ground. Coriander is an essential spice in Indian cooking and lends an aromatic flavour to soups, curries and vegetable dishes.

Cumin These small, narrow, brown seeds have an aromatic, warm, earthy flavour and are available whole or ground. Cumin is widely used in Asian and Middle Eastern cooking. The ground spice is an essential ingredient in garam masala and other spice mixes.

Cardamom pods These pale green, aromatic pods are about 1.5cm/⅝in long. Used extensively in sweet and savoury Indian dishes, cardamom is available as whole pods, seeds or ground. If using whole, lightly crush the pods to release the aroma.

Mustard seeds These brown and black seeds are an essential flavouring in Indian cooking. Add the seeds to hot oil and cook until they begin to pop and release their wonderfully nutty flavour into the oil.

Turmeric This bright yellow spice has a musky flavour and is used in a variety of savoury dishes. The flavour can be overpowering so use sparingly. Dried turmeric looks like a knobbly root and is very hard, so it is easier to buy the spice ready-ground.

▲ Turmeric

Cinnamon Warm, fragrant cinnamon is the thinly rolled bark of an evergreen tree. The spice is available whole or ground and is used to flavour rice dishes, curries and desserts.

Cloves This dark brown, nail-shaped spice is a traditional flavouring in Asian cooking. It has a very strong taste so should be used sparingly.

Saffron This expensive spice is made from the dried stigmas of the saffron crocus. It adds a vivid yellow-orange colour and a subtle, musky flavour to both sweet and savoury dishes. The saffron threads should be soaked in warm water or milk to release their colour, then added to the dish along with the soaking liquid.

Star anise This dark brown, star-shaped pod contains pea-size seeds. It has a fragrance similar to aniseed but is more robust, with hints of liquorice. It is widely used in braised dishes and desserts and is an essential ingredient in five-spice powder.

Five-spice powder This classic spice mix is widely used in Chinese cooking, particularly in braised dishes. It contains ground star anise, Sichuan peppercorns, fennel seeds, cloves and cinnamon and has a pungent, fragrant, spicy, slightly sweet flavour.

Seven-spice powder This Japanese spice blend contains ground chilli, hemp seed, poppy seed, rape seed, Sichuan peppercorns, black and white sesame seeds, and dried ground tangerine peel.

Curry powders and curry pastes There is a wide selection of ready-made spice blends and pastes for flavouring curries and other dishes. They can be found in most large supermarkets and Asian stores.

Tamarind The dried or semi-dried pulp of this pod-like fruit is used to add a sweet-sour flavour to food. It is sold in blocks or paste and should be soaked or blended with hot water before adding to dishes.

▼ Fresh tamarind pods

▲ Palm sugar

Palm sugar Made from the boiled-down sap of the palm tree, palm sugar ranges in colour from pale gold to dark brown. Sold in blocks, it is dense and crumbly and should be grated or gently melted before use. Soft brown sugar can be substituted if necessary.

Soy sauce Made from fermented soya beans, there are two main types of soy sauce: dark and light. Dark soy sauce is aged longer than the lighter varieties and is rich and dense. It is used in stews and other Chinese and Asian braised dishes, and as a dipping sauce. Light soy is lighter, thinner and saltier and is mainly used in dishes featuring pale food.

Fish sauce This thin, brown, salty sauce has a characteristic "fishy" smell and is a key ingredient in many Vietnamese, Thai, Laotian and Cambodian dishes. Made from fermented prawns (shrimp) and fish, its strong flavour diminishes when cooked with other ingredients. Fish sauce also forms the basis of Thai-style salad dressings.

Hoisin sauce This thick, sweet-spiced Chinese sauce is made from sugar, garlic, soya beans and spices. It is commonly used in stir-fries and as a dipping sauce.

Kecap manis This thick, dark, sweet soy sauce is used in Indonesian cooking and throughout South-east Asia. It can be combined with light soy sauce and other aromatics to make a rich and spicy dipping sauce.

Yellow bean sauce This thick, ochre paste is made from fermented yellow soy beans. It is used in Malaysian, Thai and Chinese cooking to flavour many vegetable and meat dishes.

Salted black beans Fermented, salted black soya beans are used to impart a distinct flavour to many Chinese dishes. The beans are available in cans or dried in packets; both types should be soaked well before use. Black bean sauce is made from a mixture of black beans, soy sauce, sugar and spices and can be bought ready-made.

Pickled ginger root Also known as *gari*, this sweet, spicy condiment is used as a garnish in Japanese cooking. Thinly sliced pieces of fresh ginger root are pickled in sweet vinegar, coloured pink. It is available in jars from large supermarkets and Asian stores.

Wasabi paste Derived from a plant native to Japan, this bright green, extremely pungent paste is made from the knobbly root and has a kick like very strong mustard. Also known as Japanese horseradish, it is used as a condiment for sushi, sashimi and other Japanese food. Use with care.

Chilli oil Made with crushed dried red chillies, this fiery, pale red oil is used as a seasoning in Asian foods. It can also be used to perk up dipping sauces.

Sesame oil This aromatic, amber-coloured, nutty-flavoured oil is made from sesame seeds. It is generally sprinkled on to food at the end of cooking as a seasoning. It has a very strong flavour so use sparingly.

Mirin This Japanese sweet rice wine is used as a salad dressing, in stir-fries and as a marinade.

Rice wine Also known as Chinese rice wine and Shoa Xing, this is an amber-coloured liquid seasoning with a rich, sweet taste, made from distilled, fermented rice. If you cannot find rice wine, dry sherry can be used instead.

Rice vinegar This pale yellow, mild, slightly sweet-tasting vinegar is made from fermented rice and is used to season food. If unavailable, you can use cider vinegar instead.

▼ Hoisin sauce, soy sauce and mirin

Basic recipes

Red curry paste

You can buy ready-made Thai red and green curry pastes from most large supermarkets, but you will get even better results if you make it yourself.

MAKES 1 SMALL JAR

6–8 fresh red chillies, seeded and sliced

15ml/1 tbsp coriander seeds, roasted

10ml/2 tsp finely grated fresh root ginger or galangal

30ml/2 tbsp finely chopped lemon grass

15ml/1 tbsp finely grated garlic

3 red shallots, finely chopped

juice of ½ small lime

30ml/2 tbsp sunflower oil

Place all the ingredients in a food processor and blend until smooth. Alternatively, place the ingredients in a large mortar and pound to a smooth paste using a pestle. Use immediately or transfer the paste to an airtight container and store in the refrigerator for up to 2 weeks.

Green curry paste

This classic Thai curry paste can be used in many dishes. Store any leftover paste in an airtight container in the refrigerator for up to 2 weeks.

MAKES 1 SMALL JAR

10–12 fresh green chillies, seeded and chopped

15ml/1 tbsp finely grated garlic

10ml/2 tsp finely grated fresh root ginger or galangal

30ml/2 tbsp chopped lemon grass

4 kaffir lime leaves, finely snipped

4 red shallots, chopped

15ml/1 tbsp coriander seeds, roasted

50g/2oz coriander (cilantro) leaves, stalks and roots, roughly chopped

5ml/1 tsp ground black pepper

rind of 1 lime, finely grated

salt, to taste

90ml/6 tbsp sunflower oil

Place all the ingredients in a food processor and blend to make a thick paste. Alternatively pound in a mortar.

Chilli sauce

This spicy, aromatic sauce can be used as a flavouring ingredient in braised dishes, stir-fries and dressings, or can be served as a dipping sauce.

MAKES 1 SMALL BOTTLE

10 fresh red chillies, seeded and chopped

4 garlic cloves, chopped

15ml/1 tbsp fish sauce

15ml/1 tbsp grated palm sugar or soft brown sugar

30ml/2 tbsp lime juice

5ml/1 tsp salt

120ml/4fl oz water

45ml/3 tbsp sunflower or groundnut (peanut) oil

Place all the ingredients in a small pan. Bring to the boil, then reduce the heat and simmer gently for 15 minutes. Transfer the mixture to a small food processor and blend until smooth. Pour the mixture into a small airtight jar or bottle and store in the refrigerator for up to 1 week.

Sweet chilli sauce

This sweet, spicy sauce has a wonderfully aromatic flavour and lovely translucent red colour. It can be used both for flavouring and as a dipping sauce. Any remaining sauce can be stored in the refrigerator in an airtight container for 1–2 weeks.

MAKES 1 SMALL BOTTLE

6 large red chillies

60ml/4 tbsp white vinegar

250g/9oz caster (superfine) sugar

5ml/1 tsp salt

4 garlic cloves, chopped

10ml/2 tsp fish sauce

Remove the seeds from the chillies and soak the seeds in hot water for about 15 minutes. Chop the chillies and place in a food processor. Drain the seeds and add to the food processor with the vinegar, sugar, salt and garlic. Blend until smooth, then transfer to a small pan and cook over a medium heat for 20 minutes, or until thickened. Leave to cool, then stir in the fish sauce.

Tamarind sauce

This sweet, tangy dipping sauce has a fruity flavour and is perfect served with spicy deep-fried snacks. The quantities here are suitable for one serving, but if there is any left over, it can be stored in the refrigerator for up to 1 week.

MAKES 1 SMALL JAR

90ml/6 tbsp tamarind paste

90ml/6 tbsp water

45ml/3 tbsp caster (superfine) sugar

Place all the ingredients in a small pan and bring the mixture to the boil. Reduce the heat and cook gently for 3–4 minutes, stirring occasionally. Remove the pan from the heat and leave to cool before serving.

Crispy fried shallots

These crisp and golden deep-fried shallots are a classic South-east Asian garnish. They have a fragrant aroma and deliciously crunchy texture and are particularly good sprinkled over stir-fries and salads. They can be stored in an airtight jar for up to 1 week.

MAKES 1 SMALL JAR

115g/4oz red shallots

oil, for deep-frying

Peel and finely slice the shallots, separating them into little rings. Fill a wok one-third full of oil and heat to 180°C/350°F. Add the shallots and fry for 1–2 minutes, or until crisp and golden. Using a wire skimmer or slotted spoon, lift the shallots from the wok and drain well on kitchen paper. Leave to cool completely, then transfer to an airtight container.

Small and bitesize

Steamed morsels, succulent snacks, golden bites and crispy mouthfuls

There's something utterly enticing about bitesize snacks and crispy morsels. What could be more sensuous than food that you can simply pop into your mouth, offering instant gratification as your teeth break through the crisp golden coating of a pakora or sink into the soft, sticky texture of a steamed dumpling? Piping hot and straight from the wok, these little mouthfuls of pleasure are perfect for parties, sensational as appetizers, and fabulous as snacks to enjoy with friends. Imagine a platter piled high with crisp, leafy little parcels of chicken, or mild, golden strips of squid spiked on pretty sticks. Dip delicately steamed rice balls into tangy, spicy sauce, then enjoy the sensation as the flavours melt together in your mouth. Or tuck into a plate of mini popadoms topped with spicy lamb and experience the crisp and juicy textures and the contrast of mild and spicy flavours as they explode on your tongue.

Pea and potato pakoras with coconut and mint chutney

These delicious golden bites are sold as street food throughout India. They make a wonderful snack drizzled with the fragrant chutney, or you could sandwich them in a crusty roll for a light lunch.

MAKES 25

15ml/1 tbsp sunflower oil

20ml/4 tsp cumin seeds

5ml/1 tsp black mustard seeds

1 small onion, finely chopped

10ml/2 tsp grated fresh root ginger

2 green chillies, seeded and chopped

600g/1lb 5oz potatoes, peeled, diced and boiled until tender

200g/7oz fresh peas

juice of 1 lemon

90ml/6 tbsp chopped fresh coriander (cilantro) leaves

115g/4oz/1 cup besan (chickpea flour)

25g/1oz/¼ cup self-raising (self-rising) flour

40g/1½oz/⅓ cup rice flour

large pinch of turmeric

10ml/2 tsp crushed coriander seeds

350ml/12fl oz/1½ cups water

vegetable oil, for frying

salt and ground black pepper

FOR THE CHUTNEY

105ml/7 tbsp coconut cream

200ml/7fl oz/scant 1 cup natural (plain) yogurt

50g/2oz mint leaves, finely chopped

5ml/1 tsp golden caster (superfine) sugar

juice of 1 lime

1 Heat a wok over a medium heat and add the sunflower oil. When hot, add the cumin and mustard seeds and stir-fry for 1–2 minutes.

2 Add the onion, ginger and chillies to the wok and cook for 3–4 minutes. Add the cooked potatoes and peas and stir-fry for 3-4 minutes. Season, then stir in the lemon juice and coriander leaves.

3 Leave the mixture to cool slightly, then divide into 25 portions. Shape each portion into a ball and chill.

4 To make the batter put the besan, self-raising flour and rice flour in a bowl. Season and add the turmeric and coriander seeds. Gradually whisk in the water to make a smooth, thick batter.

5 To make the chutney place all the ingredients in a blender and process until smooth. Season, then chill.

6 To cook the pakoras, fill a wok one-third full of oil and heat to 180°C/350°F. (A cube of bread, dropped into the oil, should brown in 15 seconds.) Working in batches, dip the balls in the batter, then drop into the oil and deep-fry for 1–2 minutes, or until golden. Drain on kitchen paper and serve with the chutney.

Besan Also known as gram flour, this fine yellow flour is made from ground chickpeas and is widely used in Asian cooking. It is available in most large supermarkets and Asian stores.

Crispy golden corn cakes with red pepper aioli

East meets West in these crisp, mouthwatering cakes that bring together creamy goat's cheese and tangy Mediterranean peppers in the Asian wok. If you're short on time, make the piquant aioli using bottled peppers instead of roasting them yourself.

SERVES 4

300g/11oz/scant 2 cups fresh corn kernels

200g/7oz/scant 1 cup ricotta cheese

200g/7oz/scant 1 cup goat's cheese, crumbled

30ml/2 tbsp thyme leaves

50g/2oz/½ cup plain (all-purpose) flour

1 large (US extra large) egg, lightly beaten

150g/5oz natural dried breadcrumbs

vegetable oil, for frying

salt and ground black pepper

FOR THE AIOLI

2 red (bell) peppers, halved and seeded

2 garlic cloves, crushed

250ml/8fl oz/1 cup mayonnaise

1 Make the aioli. Preheat the grill (broiler) to medium-high and cook the peppers, skin-side up, for 8–10 minutes, until the skins blister. Place the peppers in a plastic bag for 10 minutes and then peel away the skin. Place the flesh in a food processor with the garlic and mayonnaise and blend until fairly smooth. Transfer to a bowl and chill.

2 In a bowl, combine the corn, cheeses and thyme, then stir in the flour and egg and season well.

3 Place the breadcrumbs on a plate. Roll 15ml/1 tbsp of the corn mixture into a ball, flatten slightly and coat in the breadcrumbs. Place on baking parchment and chill for 30 minutes.

4 Fill a wok one-third full of oil and heat to 180°C/350°F (or until a cube of bread, dropped into the oil, browns in 15 seconds). Working in batches, deep-fry the corn cakes for 1–2 minutes, until golden. Drain well on kitchen paper and serve with the aioli.

Spiced noodle pancakes

The delicate rice noodles puff up in the hot oil to give a wonderfully crunchy bite that melts in the mouth. For maximum enjoyment, serve the golden pancakes as soon as they are cooked and savour the subtle blend of spices and wonderfully crisp texture.

SERVES 4

150g/5oz dried thin rice noodles	5ml/1 tsp ground cumin
1 red chilli, finely diced	5ml/1 tsp ground coriander
10ml/2 tsp garlic salt	large pinch of ground turmeric
5ml/1 tsp ground ginger	salt
¼ small red onion, very finely diced	vegetable oil, for frying
5ml/1 tsp finely chopped lemon grass	sweet chilli sauce, for dipping

1 Roughly break up the noodles and place in a large bowl. Pour over enough boiling water to cover and soak for 4–5 minutes. Drain and rinse under cold water. Dry on kitchen paper.

2 Transfer the noodles to a bowl and add the chilli, garlic salt, ground ginger, red onion, lemon grass, ground cumin, coriander and turmeric. Toss well to mix and season with salt.

3 Heat 5–6cm/2–2½in oil in a wok. Working in batches, drop tablespoons of the noodle mixture into the oil. Flatten using the back of a skimmer and cook for 1–2 minutes on each side until crisp and golden. Drain on kitchen paper and serve with the chilli sauce.

Steamed crab dim sum with Chinese chives

These delectable Chinese-style dumplings have a wonderfully sticky texture and make a perfect appetizer. You can make them in advance, storing them in the refrigerator until ready to cook. Steam them just before serving, then enjoy the sensation as your teeth sink through the soft wrapper into the filling.

SERVES 4

150g/5oz fresh white crab meat

115g/4oz minced (ground) pork

30ml/2 tbsp chopped Chinese chives

15ml/1 tbsp finely chopped red (bell) pepper

30ml/2 tbsp sweet chilli sauce

30ml/2 tbsp hoisin sauce

24 fresh dumpling wrappers (available from Asian stores)

Chinese chives, to garnish

chilli oil and soy sauce, to serve

1 Place the crab meat, pork and chopped chives in a bowl. Add the red pepper, sweet chilli and hoisin sauces and mix well to combine.

2 Working with 2–3 wrappers at a time, put a small spoonful of the mixture into the centre of each wrapper.

3 Brush the edges of each wrapper with water and fold over to form a half-moon shape. Press and pleat the edges to seal and tap the base of each dumpling to flatten. Cover with a clean, damp cloth and make the remaining dumplings in the same way.

4 Arrange the dumplings on 1–3 lightly oiled plates and fit inside 1–3 tiers of a bamboo steamer.

5 Cover the steamer and place over a wok of simmering water (making sure the water does not touch the steamer). Steam for 8–10 minutes, or until the dumplings are cooked through and become slightly translucent.

6 Divide the dumplings among four plates and serve immediately garnished with Chinese chives and chilli oil and soy sauce for dipping.

Prawn dim sum To make a delicious variation on these crab dim sum, try using chopped raw tiger prawns (jumbo shrimp) in place of the crab.

Steamed oysters with zesty tomato and cucumber salsa

A plate of lightly steamed fresh oysters makes a delicious appetizer for a special occasion. The fresh, zesty, aromatic salsa complements the delicate flavour and texture of the oysters perfectly and each irresistible mouthful feels like the ultimate indulgence.

SERVES 4

12–16 oysters

30ml/2 tbsp sunflower oil

1 garlic clove, crushed

15ml/1 tbsp light soy sauce

sea salt, to serve

FOR THE SALSA

1 ripe plum tomato

½ small cucumber

¼ small red onion

15ml/1 tbsp very finely chopped coriander (cilantro)

1 small red chilli, seeded and very finely chopped

juice of 1–2 limes

salt and ground black pepper

1 First prepare the salsa. Halve the tomato and remove the seeds, then finely dice the tomato, cucumber and red onion. Place in a bowl with the chopped coriander and red chilli. Add the lime juice and season to taste. Set aside (at room temperature) for 15–20 minutes.

2 Carefully open the oysters using a special oyster knife or a strong knife with a short, blunt blade.

3 Arrange the oysters in their half shells in a bamboo steamer (using several tiers if necessary). Mix together the sunflower oil, garlic and soy sauce and spoon over the oysters.

4 Cover the steamer and place over a wok of simmering water (making sure it does not touch the water). Steam the oysters for 2–3 minutes, or until they are just slightly firm on the outside. Arrange on a bed of sea salt, top each oyster with a small spoonful of the salsa and serve immediately.

Crispy salt and pepper squid

These delicious morsels of squid look stunning skewered on small or large wooden sticks and are perfect served with drinks, or as an appetizer. The crisp, golden coating contrasts perfectly with the succulent squid inside, and they taste divine dipped into sweet-and-sour sauce or piquant chilli sauce. Serve piping hot straight from the wok.

SERVES 4

750g/1lb 10oz fresh squid, cleaned

juice of 4–5 lemons

15ml/1 tbsp freshly ground black pepper

15ml/1 tbsp sea salt

10ml/2 tsp caster (superfine) sugar

115g/4oz/1 cup cornflour (cornstarch)

3 egg whites, lightly beaten

vegetable oil, for frying

chilli sauce or sweet-and-sour sauce, for dipping

skewers or toothpicks, to serve

1 Cut the squid into large bitesize pieces and score a diamond pattern on each piece.

2 Trim the tentacles. Place in a large mixing bowl and pour over the lemon juice. Cover and marinate for 10–15 minutes. Drain well and pat dry.

3 In a separate bowl mix together the pepper, salt, sugar and cornflour. Dip the squid pieces in the egg white and then toss lightly in the seasoned flour, shaking off any excess.

4 Fill a wok one-third full of oil and heat to 180°C/350°F. (A cube of bread, dropped into the oil, should brown in 15 seconds.) Working in batches, deep-fry the squid for 1 minute. Drain on kitchen paper and serve threaded on to skewers with chilli or sweet-and-sour sauce.

Cleaning squid Pull the head and tentacles away from the body; the intestines and quill should pull away at the same time. Pull off the purplish membrane from the body, then slit the body open and wash under cold water.

Salmon, sesame and ginger fishcakes

These light fishcakes are scented with the exotic flavours of sesame, lime and ginger. They make a tempting appetizer served simply with a wedge of lime for squeezing over, but are also perfect for a light lunch or supper, served with a crunchy, refreshing salad.

MAKES 25

500g/1¼lb salmon fillet, skinned and boned

45ml/3 tbsp dried breadcrumbs

30ml/2 tbsp mayonnaise

30ml/2 tbsp sesame seeds

30ml/2 tbsp light soy sauce

finely grated zest of 2 limes

10ml/2 tsp finely grated fresh root ginger

4 spring onions (scallions), finely sliced

vegetable oil, for frying

salt and ground black pepper

spring onion slivers, to garnish

lime wedges, to serve

1 Finely chop the salmon and place in a bowl. Add the breadcrumbs, mayonnaise, sesame seeds, soy sauce, lime zest, ginger and spring onions and use your fingers to mix well.

2 With wet hands, divide the mixture into 25 portions and shape each one into a small round cake.

3 Place the cakes on a baking sheet, lined with baking parchment, cover and chill for several hours or overnight.

4 When you are ready to cook the fishcakes heat about 5cm/2in vegetable oil in a wok.

5 Working in batches, shallow fry the fishcakes over a medium heat for 2–3 minutes on each side.

6 Drain the fishcakes well on kitchen paper and serve warm or at room temperature, garnished with spring onion slivers and plenty of lime wedges for squeezing over.

Seaweed-wrapped prawn and water chestnut rolls

Japanese nori seaweed is used to enclose the fragrant filling of prawns, water chestnuts and fresh herbs and spices in these pretty steamed rolls. Ideal for entertaining, the rolls can be prepared in advance and stored in the refrigerator until ready to steam.

SERVES 4

675g/1½lb raw tiger prawns (shrimp), peeled and deveined

5ml/1 tsp finely chopped kaffir lime leaves

1 red chilli, seeded and chopped

5ml/1 tsp finely grated garlic clove

5ml/1 tsp finely grated root ginger

5ml/1 tsp finely grated lime zest

60ml/4 tbsp very finely chopped fresh coriander (cilantro)

1 egg white, lightly beaten

30ml/2 tbsp chopped water chestnuts

4 sheets of nori

salt and ground black pepper

ketjap manis or soy sauce, to serve

1 Place the prawns in a food processor with the lime leaves, red chilli, garlic, ginger, lime zest and coriander. Process until smooth, add the egg white and water chestnuts, season and process until combined. Transfer the mixture to a bowl, cover and chill for 3–4 hours.

2 Lay the nori sheets on a clean, dry surface and spread the prawn mixture over each sheet, leaving a 2cm/¾in border at one end. Roll up to form tight rolls, wrap in clear film (plastic wrap) and chill for 2–3 hours.

3 Unwrap the rolls and place on a board. Using a sharp knife, cut each roll into 2cm/¾in lengths. Place the slices in a baking parchment-lined bamboo steamer, cover and place over a wok of simmering water (making sure the water does not touch the steamer). Steam for 6–8 minutes, or until cooked through. Serve warm or at room temperature with ketjap manis or soy sauce.

Steamed rice balls with spicy dipping sauce

Bitesize balls of steamed pork and mushrooms rolled in jasmine rice make a fabulous snack to serve with pre-dinner drinks, or as part of a selection of dim sum.

SERVES 4

30ml/2 tbsp oil

200g/7oz/scant 3 cups finely chopped shiitake mushrooms

400g/14oz minced (ground) pork

4 spring onions (scallions), chopped

2 garlic cloves, crushed

15ml/1 tbsp fish sauce

15ml/1 tbsp soy sauce

15ml/1 tsp grated fresh root ginger

60ml/4 tbsp finely chopped coriander (cilantro)

1 egg, lightly beaten

salt and ground black pepper

200g/7oz/1 cup jasmine rice

FOR THE DIPPING SAUCE

120ml/4fl oz/½ cup sweet chilli sauce

105ml/7 tbsp soy sauce

15ml/1 tbsp Chinese rice wine

5–10ml/1–2 tsp chilli oil

1 Heat the oil in a large wok, then add the mushrooms and stir-fry over a high heat for 2–3 minutes. Transfer to a food processor with the pork, spring onions, garlic, fish sauce, soy sauce, ginger, coriander and beaten egg. Process for 30–40 seconds, transfer to a bowl and combine well by hand. Cover and chill in the fridge for 3–4 hours or overnight.

2 To cook, place the rice in a bowl. With wet hands, divide the mushroom mixture into 20 portions and roll each one into a firm ball. Roll each ball in the rice then arrange the balls, spaced apart, in two baking parchment-lined tiers of a bamboo steamer.

3 Cover the steamer and place over a wok of simmering water. Steam for 1 hour 15 minutes. (Check the water often, replenishing when necessary.)

4 Meanwhile, combine all the dipping sauce ingredients in a small bowl.

5 When the balls are cooked, remove from the steamer and serve warm or at room temperature with the bowl of spicy dipping sauce.

Scented garlic chicken wrapped in pandanus leaves

Dark green panadanus leaves are available from Chinese and Asian supermarkets and are similar to bamboo leaves. They impart a wonderfully fragrant flavour to the chicken but should be removed before eating. You can use lightly oiled foil instead if you prefer.

SERVES 4

400g/14oz boneless, skinless chicken thighs

45ml/3 tbsp soy sauce

30ml/2 tbsp finely grated garlic

15ml/1 tbsp cumin

15ml/1 tbsp ground coriander

15ml/1 tbsp golden caster (superfine) sugar

5ml/1 tsp finely grated fresh root ginger

1 bird's eye chilli

30ml/2 tbsp oyster sauce

15ml/1 tbsp fish sauce

a bunch of pandanus leaves, to wrap

vegetable oil, for frying

sweet chilli sauce, to serve

1 Cut the chicken into bitesize pieces and place in a large mixing bowl.

2 Place the soy sauce, garlic, cumin, coriander, sugar, ginger, chilli, oyster sauce and fish sauce in a blender and process until smooth. Pour over the chicken, cover and leave to marinate in the refrigerator for 6-8 hours.

3 When ready to cook, drain the chicken from the marinade and wrap each piece in a pandanus leaf (you will need to cut the leaves to size using scissors) and secure each one with a cocktail stick (toothpick).

4 Fill a wok one-third full of oil and heat to 180°C/350°F (or until a cube of bread, dropped into the oil, browns in 15 seconds). Carefully add the chicken parcels, 3–4 at a time, and deep-fry for 3–4 minutes, or until cooked through. Drain on kitchen paper and serve with the chilli sauce. (Do not eat the leaves!)

Fragrant coconut spiced lamb on mini poppadums

Crisp, melt-in-the-mouth mini poppadums make a great base for these divine little bites. Top them with a drizzle of yogurt and a spoonful of mango chutney, then serve immediately. To make an equally tasty variation, you can use chicken or pork in place of the lamb.

MAKES 25

30ml/2 tbsp sunflower oil

4 shallots, finely chopped

30ml/2 tbsp medium curry paste

300g/11oz minced (ground) lamb

90ml/6 tbsp tomato purée (paste)

5ml/1 tsp caster (superfine) sugar

200ml/7fl oz/scant 1 cup coconut cream

juice of 1 lime

60ml/4 tbsp chopped fresh mint leaves

25 mini poppadums

vegetable oil, for frying

salt and ground black pepper

natural (plain) yogurt and mango chutney, to drizzle

red chilli slivers and mint leaves, to garnish

1 Heat the oil in a wok over a medium heat and add the shallots. Stir fry for 4–5 minutes, until softened, then add the curry paste. Stir-fry for 1–2 minutes and then add the lamb. Stir-fry over a high heat for a further 4–5 minutes, then stir in the tomato purée, sugar and coconut cream.

2 Cook the lamb over a gentle heat for 25–30 minutes, or until the meat is tender and all the liquid has been absorbed. Season and stir in the lime juice and mint leaves. Remove from the heat and keep warm.

3 Fill a separate wok one-third full of oil and deep-fry the mini poppadums for 30–40 seconds, until puffed up and crisp. Drain on kitchen paper.

4 Place the poppadums on a serving platter. Put a spoonful of spiced lamb on each one, then top with a little yogurt and mango chutney. Serve immediately, garnished with slivers of red chilli and mint leaves.

Golden beef and potato puffs

These crisp, golden pillows of pastry filled with spiced beef and potatoes are delicious served piping hot, straight from the wok. The light, flaky pastry puffs up wonderfully in the hot oil and contrasts enticingly with the fragrant spiced beef within. Serve as a snack with drinks, or as an appetizer for an informal dinner.

SERVES 4

15ml/1 tbsp sunflower oil

½ small onion, finely chopped

3 garlic cloves, crushed

5ml/1 tsp finely grated fresh root ginger

1 red chilli, seeded and finely chopped

30ml/2 tbsp hot curry powder

75g/3oz minced (ground) beef

115g/4oz mashed potato

60ml/4 tbsp chopped fresh coriander (cilantro)

2 sheets ready-rolled, fresh puff pastry

1 egg, lightly beaten

vegetable oil, for frying

salt and ground black pepper

fresh coriander leaves, to garnish

tomato ketchup, to serve

1 Heat the oil in a wok, then add the onion, garlic, ginger and chilli. Stir-fry over a medium heat for 2–3 minutes. Add the curry powder and beef and stir-fry over a high heat for a further 4–5 minutes, or until the beef is browned and just cooked through, then remove from the heat.

2 Transfer the beef mixture to a large bowl and add the mashed potato and chopped fresh coriander. Stir well, then season and set aside.

3 Lay the pastry sheets on a clean, dry surface and cut out 8 rounds, using a 7.5cm/3in pastry (cookie) cutter.

4 Place a large spoonful of the beef mixture in the centre of each pastry round. Brush the edges of the pastry with the beaten egg and fold each round in half to enclose the filling. Press and crimp the edges with the tines of a fork to seal.

5 Fill a wok one-third full of oil and heat to 180°C/350°F (or until a cube of bread, dropped into the oil, browns in 15 seconds).

6 Deep-fry the puffs, in batches, for 2–3 minutes until puffed up and golden brown. Drain on kitchen paper and serve garnished with fresh coriander leaves. Offer a small bowl of tomato ketchup for dipping.

Crisp golden crescents For a change in texture, you can use ready-made shortcrust pastry in place of the puff pastry. The puffs will be transformed into little golden crescents with a firmer, crisper shell and the same succulent beef filling.

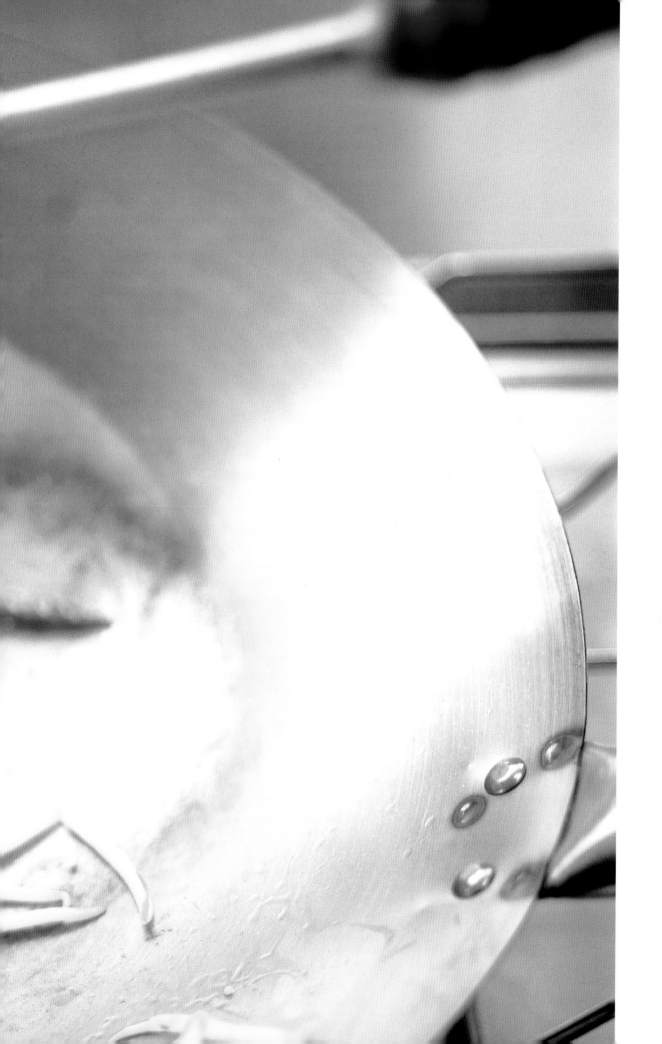

Fresh flavours, crunchy texures, fragrant salads and speedy stir-fries

There is little more delicious than gloriously fresh ingredients, cooked to perfection so that you can still taste their just-harvested flavours. This chapter is packed with fantastic ideas for searing, steaming and stir-frying. Each one uses fabulously fresh ingredients – from crisp and crunchy vegetables to delectable fish and shellfish – and pairs them with zingy, zesty flavourings that will set your tastebuds aquiver. After a busy day at work, toss together a speedy stir-fry such as tiger prawns with cucumber and dill, or jewelled vegetable rice with crispy deep-fried eggs. Or when you're entertaining, offer your guests sumptuous delights such as herb- and chilli-seared scallops on wilted pak choi or aromatic pork with basil, mushrooms and mangetout, which you can cook in minutes.

Sesame-tossed asparagus with crispy bean thread noodles

Tender asparagus spears tossed with sesame seeds and served on a bed of crispy, deep-fried noodles makes a lovely dish for casual entertaining. The lightly cooked asparagus retains all its fresh flavour and bite, which contrasts wonderfully with the crunchy noodles.

SERVES 4

15ml/1 tbsp sunflower oil

350g/12oz thin asparagus spears

5ml/1 tsp salt

5ml/1 tsp freshly ground black pepper

5ml/1 tsp golden caster (superfine) sugar

30ml/2 tbsp Chinese cooking wine

45ml/3 tbsp light soy sauce

60ml/4 tbsp oyster sauce

10ml/2 tsp sesame oil

60ml/4 tbsp toasted sesame seeds

FOR THE NOODLES

50g/2oz dried bean thread noodles or thin rice noodles

sunflower oil, for frying

1 First make the crispy noodles. Fill a wok one-third full of oil and heat to 180°C/350°F (or until a cube of bread, dropped into the oil, browns in 15 seconds). Add the noodles, small bunches at a time, to the oil; they will crisp and puff up in seconds. Using a slotted spoon, remove from the wok and drain on kitchen paper. Set aside.

2 Heat a clean wok over a high heat and add the sunflower oil. Add the asparagus and stir-fry for 3 minutes.

3 Add the salt, pepper, sugar, wine and both sauces to the wok and stir-fry for 2–3 minutes. Add the sesame oil, toss to combine and remove from the heat.

4 To serve, divide the crispy noodles between 4 warmed plates or bowls and top with the asparagus and juices. Scatter over the toasted sesame seeds and serve immediately.

Aromatic chilli-spiced okra and coconut stir-fry

Quick, stir-fried okra spiced with mustard, cumin and red chillies and sprinkled with freshly grated coconut makes a great quick supper. It is the perfect way to enjoy these succulent dark green pods, with the sweetness of the coconut complementing the warm spices perfectly.

SERVES 4

600g/1lb 6oz okra

60ml/4 tbsp sunflower oil

1 onion, finely chopped

15ml/1 tbsp mustard seeds

15ml/1 tbsp cumin seeds

2–3 dried red chillies

10–12 curry leaves

2.5ml/½ tsp turmeric

90g/3½oz freshly grated coconut

salt and ground black pepper

poppadums, rice or naan, to serve

1 Using a sharp knife, cut the okra diagonally into 1cm/½in lengths, then set aside.

2 Heat the sunflower oil in a wok. When hot add the chopped onion and stir-fry over a medium heat for about 5 minutes until softened.

3 Add the mustard seeds, cumin seeds, red chillies and curry leaves to the onions and stir-fry over a high heat for about 2 minutes.

4 Add the okra and turmeric to the wok and continue to stir-fry over a high heat for 3–4 minutes.

5 Remove the wok from the heat, sprinkle over the coconut and season well with salt and ground black pepper. Serve immediately with poppadums, steamed rice or naan bread.

Buying okra Fresh okra is widely available from most supermarkets and Asian stores. Choose fresh, firm, green specimens and avoid any that are soft or turning brown.

Noodle, tofu and sprouted bean salad

This crisp and refreshing salad is ultra-quick to make and is bursting with the goodness of fresh vegetables and the fragrant flavour of herbs, rice vinegar and peppery chilli oil. Fresh sprouted beans are available from most supermarkets, but you can easily sprout them yourself at home.

SERVES 4

25g/1oz bean thread noodles

500g/1¼lb mixed sprouted beans and pulses (aduki, chickpea, mung, red lentil)

4 spring onions (scallions), finely shredded

115g/4oz firm tofu, diced

1 ripe plum tomato, seeded and diced

½ cucumber, peeled, seeded and diced

60ml/4 tbsp chopped fresh coriander (cilantro)

45ml/3 tbsp chopped fresh mint

60ml/4 tbsp rice vinegar

10ml/2 tsp caster (superfine) sugar

10ml/2 tsp sesame oil

5ml/1 tsp chilli oil

salt and ground black pepper

1 Place the bean thread noodles in a bowl and pour over enough boiling water to cover. Leave to soak for 12–15 minutes and then drain and refresh under cold, running water and drain again. Using a pair of scissors, cut the noodles roughly into 7.5cm/3in lengths and set aside.

2 Fill a wok one-third full of boiling water and place over a high heat. Add the sprouted beans and pulses and blanch for 1 minute. Drain, return to the wok and add the spring onions, tofu, tomato, cucumber and herbs.

3 Combine the rice vinegar, sugar, sesame oil and chilli oil and toss into the noodle mixture. Transfer to a bowl and chill for 30 minutes before serving.

Jewelled vegetable rice with crispy deep-fried eggs

Inspired by the traditional Indonesian dish *nasi goreng*, this vibrant, colourful stir-fry makes a tasty light meal. Alternatively, serve it as an accompaniment to simply grilled meat or fish. To make an extra-healthy option, use brown basmati rice in place of the white rice.

SERVES 4

30ml/2 tbsp sunflower oil

2 garlic cloves, finely chopped

4 red Asian shallots, thinly sliced

1 small red chilli, finely sliced

90g/3½oz carrots, cut into thin matchsticks

90g/3½oz fine green beans, cut into 2cm/¾in lengths

90g/3½oz fresh corn kernels

1 red (bell) pepper, seeded and cut into 1cm/½in dice

90g/3½oz baby button (white) mushrooms

500g/1¼lb cooked, cooled long grain rice

45ml/3 tbsp light soy sauce

10ml/2 tsp green Thai curry paste

4 crispy fried eggs, to serve

crisp green salad leaves and lime wedges, to garnish

1 Heat the sunflower oil in a wok over a high heat. When hot, add the garlic, shallots and chilli. Stir-fry for about 2 minutes.

2 Add the carrots, green beans, corn, red pepper and mushrooms to the wok and stir-fry for 3–4 minutes. Add the cooked, cooled rice and stir-fry for a further 4–5 minutes.

3 Mix together the light soy sauce and curry paste and add to the wok. Toss to mix well and stir-fry for 2–3 minutes until piping hot. Ladle the rice into four bowls or plates and top each portion with a crispy fried egg. Serve with crisp green salad leaves and wedges of lime to squeeze over.

Perfect rice When making this dish, it is better to use cold cooked rice rather than hot, freshly cooked rice. Hot boiled rice tends to clump together when stir-frying, whereas the grains of cooled rice will remain separate.

Light and fragrant tiger prawns with cucumber and dill

This simple, elegant dish has a fresh, light flavour and is equally good served as a simple supper or for a dinner party. The delicate flavour of fresh prawns goes really well with mild cucumber and fragrant dill, but if you prefer a more robust dish, toss in a handful of chives as well.

SERVES 4

500g/1¼lb raw tiger prawns (jumbo shrimp), peeled with tail on

500g/1¼lb cucumber

30ml/2 tbsp butter

15ml/1 tbsp olive oil

15ml/1 tbsp finely chopped garlic

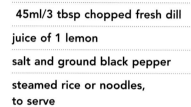

45ml/3 tbsp chopped fresh dill

juice of 1 lemon

salt and ground black pepper

steamed rice or noodles, to serve

1 Using a small, sharp knife, carefully make a shallow slit along the back of each prawn and use the point of the knife to remove the black vein. Set the prawns aside.

2 Peel the cucumber and slice in half lengthways. Using a small teaspoon, gently scoop out all the seeds and discard. Cut the cucumber into 4 x 1cm/1½ x ½in sticks.

3 Heat a wok over a high heat, then add the butter and oil. When the butter has melted, add the cucumber and garlic and stir-fry over a high heat for 2–3 minutes.

4 Add the prepared prawns to the wok and continue to stir-fry over a high heat for 3–4 minutes, or until the prawns turn pink and are just cooked through, then remove from the heat.

5 Add the fresh dill and lemon juice to the wok and toss to combine. Season well with salt and ground black pepper and serve immediately with steamed rice or noodles.

Stir-fried clams with orange and garlic

Zesty orange and pungent garlic and shallots are surprisingly good partners for sweet-tasting clams. The fresh, plump shellfish release their juices during cooking, so serve this tangy dish with plenty of crusty bread to mop up the delicious juices.

SERVES 4

1kg/2¼lb fresh clams

15ml/1 tbsp sunflower oil

30ml/2 tbsp finely chopped garlic

4 shallots, finely chopped

105ml/7 tbsp vegetable or fish stock

finely grated zest and
juice of 1 orange

salt and ground black pepper

a large handful of roughly
chopped flat leaf parsley

1 Wash and scrub the clams under cold running water. Check carefully and discard any that are open and do not close when tapped lightly.

2 Heat a wok over a high heat and add the sunflower oil. When hot, add the garlic, shallots and clams and stir-fry for 4–5 minutes.

3 Add the stock and orange zest and juice to the wok and season well. Cover and cook for 3–4 minutes, or until all the clams have opened. (Discard any unopened clams.) Stir in the chopped flat leaf parsley, remove from the heat and serve immediately.

Freshness To avoid the risk of food poisoning, it is essential that the clams are live before cooking. Tap any open clams gently with the back of a knife. Any that do not close are dead and so must be discarded; and any that remain closed after cooking should also be thrown away.

Herb- and chilli-seared scallops on wilted pak choi

Tender, succulent scallops are simply divine marinated in fresh chilli, fragrant mint and aromatic basil, then quickly seared in a piping hot wok. If you can't find king scallops for this recipe, use twice the quantity of smaller queen scallops.

SERVES 4

20–24 king scallops, cleaned

120ml/4fl oz/½ cup olive oil

finely grated zest and juice of 1 lemon

30ml/2 tbsp finely chopped mixed mint and basil

1 red chilli, seeded and finely chopped

salt and ground black pepper

500g/1¼lb pak choi (bok choy)

1 Place the scallops in a shallow, non-metallic bowl in a single layer. In a clean bowl, mix together half the oil, the lemon zest and juice, chopped herbs and chilli and spoon over the scallops. Season well with salt and black pepper, cover and set aside.

2 Using a sharp knife, cut each pak choi lengthways into four pieces.

3 Heat a wok over a high heat. When hot, drain the scallops (reserving the marinade) and add to the wok. Cook for 1 minute on each side, or until cooked to your liking.

4 Pour the marinade over the scallops and remove the wok from the heat. Transfer the scallops and juices to a platter and keep warm.

5 Wipe out the wok with a piece of kitchen paper and place the wok over a high heat. Add the remaining oil and add the pak choi. Stir-fry over a high heat for 2–3 minutes, until the leaves are wilted. Divide the greens among four warmed serving plates, then top with the reserved scallops and their juices and serve immediately.

Thai-style steamed mussels in coconut milk

Mussels steamed in coconut milk and fresh aromatic herbs and spices make an ideal dish for informal entertaining. It's quick and easy to prepare and is great for a relaxed dinner with friends. Serve with plenty of crusty bread so you can mop up the fragrant coconut milk sauce. When you make a dish that tastes this good, you and your guests won't want to leave any of it on their plates.

SERVES 4

15ml/1 tbsp sunflower oil

6 garlic cloves, roughly chopped

15ml/1 tbsp finely chopped fresh root ginger

2 large red chillies, seeded and finely sliced

6 spring onions (scallions), finely chopped

400ml/14fl oz/1⅔ cups coconut milk

45ml/3 tbsp light soy sauce

finely grated zest and juice of 2 limes

5ml/1 tsp caster (superfine) sugar

1.6kg/3½lb mussels, scrubbed and beards removed

a large handful of chopped coriander (cilantro)

salt and ground black pepper

1 Heat the wok over a high heat and then add the oil. Stir in the garlic, ginger, chillies and spring onions and stir-fry for 30 seconds.

2 Add the coconut milk, soy sauce, lime and sugar to the wok and stir to mix.

3 Bring the mixture to the boil, then add the mussels. Return to the boil, cover and cook briskly for 5–6 minutes, or until all the mussels have opened. Discard any unopened mussels.

4 Remove the wok from the heat and stir in the chopped coriander.

5 Season the mussels well with salt and pepper. Ladle into warmed bowls and serve immediately.

Keeping it casual For an informal supper with friends, take the wok straight to the table. A wok makes a great serving dish, and there's something utterly irresistible about eating straight from the pan.

Steamed fish skewers on herbed rice noodles

Fresh trout is perfect for summer entertaining. In this recipe, succulent fillets are marinated in a tangy citrus spice blend, then skewered and steamed before serving on a bed of fragrant herb noodles. The delicate noodles and richly flavoured fish make excellent partners.

SERVES 4

4 trout fillets, skinned

2.5ml/½ tsp turmeric

15ml/1 tbsp mild curry paste

juice of 2 lemons

15ml/1 tbsp sunflower oil

salt and ground black pepper

45ml/3 tbsp chilli-roasted peanuts, roughly chopped

chopped fresh mint, to garnish

FOR THE NOODLES

300g/11oz rice noodles

15ml/1 tbsp sunflower oil

1 red chilli, seeded and finely sliced

4 spring onions (scallions), cut into slivers

60ml/4 tbsp roughly chopped fresh mint

60ml/4 tbsp roughly chopped fresh sweet basil

1 Trim each fillet and place in a large bowl. Mix together the turmeric, curry paste, lemon juice and oil and pour over the fish. Season with salt and black pepper and toss to mix well.

2 Place the rice noodles in a bowl and pour over enough boiling water to cover. Leave to soak for 3–4 minutes and then drain. Refresh in cold water, drain and set aside.

3 Thread 2 bamboo skewers through each trout fillet and arrange in two tiers of a baking bamboo steamer lined with baking parchment.

4 Cover the steamer and place over a wok of simmering water (making sure the water doesn't touch the steamer). Steam the fish skewers for 5–6 minutes, or until the fish is just cooked through.

5 Meanwhile, in a clean wok heat the oil. Add the chilli, spring onions and drained noodles and stir-fry for about 2 minutes and then stir in the chopped herbs. Season with salt and ground black pepper and divide among four bowls or plates.

6 Top each bowl of noodles with a steamed fish skewer and scatter over the chilli-roasted peanuts. Garnish with chopped mint and serve immediately.

Bamboo skewers Soak the bamboo skewers in cold water for at least 30 minutes before threading them through the trout fillets. This will prevent them burning during cooking.

Crispy five-spice chicken with crunchy vegetable noodles

Tender strips of chicken fillet, with a delicately spiced rice flour coating, become deliciously crisp and golden when fried. They make a great meal served on a bed of stir-fried vegetable noodles.

SERVES 4

200g/7oz thin egg noodles

30ml/2 tbsp sunflower oil

2 garlic cloves, very thinly sliced

1 red chilli, seeded and sliced

½ red (bell) pepper, very thinly sliced

300g/11oz carrots, peeled and cut into thin strips

300g/11oz Chinese broccoli or Chinese greens, roughly sliced

45ml/3 tbsp hoisin sauce

45ml/3 tbsp soy sauce

15ml/1 tbsp caster (superfine) sugar

4 chicken breast fillets, skinned and cut into strips

2 egg whites, lightly beaten

115g/4oz/1 cup rice flour

15ml/1 tbsp five-spice powder

salt and ground black pepper

vegetable oil, for frying

1 Cook the noodles according to the packet instructions, drain and set aside.

2 Heat the sunflower oil in a wok, then add the garlic, chilli, red pepper, carrots and broccoli or greens and stir-fry over a high heat for 2–3 minutes.

3 Add the sauces and sugar to the wok and cook for a further 2–3 minutes. Add the drained noodles, toss to combine, then remove from the heat, cover and keep warm.

4 Dip the chicken strips into the egg white. Combine the rice flour and five-spice powder in a shallow dish and season. Add the chicken strips to the flour mixture and toss to coat.

5 Heat about 2.5cm/1½in oil in a clean wok. When hot, shallow fry the chicken for 3–4 minutes until crisp and golden.

6 To serve divide the noodle mixture between warmed plates or bowls and top each serving with the chicken.

Aromatic pork with basil, mushrooms and mangetout

The combination of moist, juicy pork and mushrooms, crisp green mangetout and fragrant basil in this ginger- and garlic-infused stir-fry is absolutely delicious. Served with simple steamed jasmine rice, it makes a perfect quick supper during the week.

SERVES 4

40g/1½oz cornflour (cornstarch)

500g/1¼lb pork fillet, thinly sliced

15ml/1 tbsp sunflower oil

10ml/2 tsp sesame oil

15ml/1 tbsp very finely shredded fresh root ginger

3 garlic cloves, thinly sliced

200g/7oz mangetout (snow peas), halved lengthways

300g/11oz/generous 4 cups mixed mushrooms, such as shiitake, button (white) or oyster, sliced if large

120ml/4fl oz/½ cup Chinese cooking wine

45ml/3 tbsp soy sauce

a small handful of sweet basil leaves

salt and ground black pepper

steamed jasmine rice, to serve

1 Place the cornflour in a strong plastic bag. Season well with salt and black pepper and add the sliced pork. Shake the bag to coat the pork in flour and then remove the pork and shake off any excess flour. Set aside.

2 Put the sunflower oil and sesame oil in a wok and place over a high heat. Stir in the ginger and garlic and cook for 30 seconds. Add the pork and cook over a high heat for about 5 minutes, stirring often, until sealed.

3 Add the mangetout and mushrooms to the wok and stir-fry for 2–3 minutes. Add the Chinese cooking wine and soy sauce, stir-fry for 2–3 minutes and remove from the heat.

4 Just before serving, stir the sweet basil leaves into the pork. Serve with steamed jasmine rice.

Warm lamb and noodle salad with fresh mint

This Thai-inspired salad combines thin slices of lamb with lightly cooked fresh vegetables and rice noodles, all tossed together with a deliciously fragrant, aromatic Asian-style dressing.

SERVES 4

30ml/2 tbsp red Thai curry paste

60ml/4 tbsp sunflower oil

750g/1lb 11oz lamb neck fillets, thinly sliced

250g/9oz sugar snap peas

500g/1¼lb medium or thick fresh rice noodles

1 red (bell) pepper, seeded and very thinly sliced

1 cucumber, cut into very thin slices with a vegetable peeler

6–7 spring onions (scallions), sliced diagonally

a large handful of fresh mint leaves

FOR THE DRESSING

15ml/1 tbsp sunflower oil

juice of 2 limes

1 garlic clove, crushed

15ml/1 tbsp golden caster (superfine) sugar

15ml/1 tbsp fish sauce

30ml/2 tbsp soy sauce

1 In a shallow dish, mix together the red curry paste and half the oil. Add the lamb slices and toss to coat. Cover and leave to marinate in the refrigerator for up to 24 hours.

2 Blanch the sugar snap peas in a wok of lightly salted boiling water for 1–2 minutes. Drain, refresh under cold water, drain again thoroughly and transfer to a large bowl.

3 Put the noodles in a separate bowl and pour over boiling water to cover. Leave to soak for 5–10 minutes, until tender, then drain well and separate with your fingers.

4 Add the noodles to the sugar snap peas, then add the sliced red pepper, cucumber and spring onions.

5 Heat a wok over a high heat and add the remaining sunflower oil. Stir-fry the lamb, in 2 batches, for 3–4 minutes, or until cooked through, then add to the bowl of salad ingredients.

6 Place all the dressing ingredients in a screw-top jar, screw on the lid and shake well to combine. Pour the dressing over the warm salad, sprinkle over the fresh mint leaves and toss well to combine. Serve immediately.

Warm beef salad You can make this salad using beef, if you prefer. Use thinly sliced fillet (beef tenderloin) or rump (round) steak in place of the lamb. You can also vary the herbs used. Try fresh coriander (cilantro) in place of the mint.

Beef and butternut squash with chilli and herbs

Stir-fried beef and sweet, orange-fleshed squash flavoured with warm spices, oyster sauce and fresh herbs makes a robust main couse when served with rice or egg noodles. The addition of chilli and fresh root ginger gives the dish a wonderfully vigourous bite.

SERVES 4

30ml/2 tbsp sunflower oil

2 onions, cut into thick slices

500g/1¼lb butternut squash, peeled, seeded and cut into thin strips

675g/1½lb fillet steak (beef tenderloin)

60ml/4 tbsp soy sauce

90g/3½oz/½ cup golden caster (superfine) sugar

1 bird's eye chilli, seeded and chopped

15ml/1 tbsp finely shredded fresh root ginger

30ml/2 tbsp fish sauce

5ml/1 tsp ground star anise

5ml/1 tsp five-spice powder

15ml/1 tbsp oyster sauce

4 spring onions (scallions), shredded

a small handful of sweet basil leaves

a small handful of mint leaves

1 Heat a wok over a medium-high heat and add the oil. When hot, stir in the onions and squash. Stir-fry for 2–3 minutes, then reduce the heat, cover and cook gently for 5–6 minutes, or until just tender.

2 Place the beef between 2 sheets of clear film (plastic wrap) and beat, with a mallet or rolling pin, until thin. Using a sharp knife, cut into thin strips.

3 Meanwhile, in a separate wok, add the soy sauce, sugar, chilli, ginger, fish sauce, star anise, five-spice powder and oyster sauce. Stir-fry over a medium heat for 3–4 minutes.

4 Add the beef strips to the wok and cook over a high heat for 3–4 minutes, or until cooked through. Remove from the heat.

5 Add the onion and squash slices to the beef and toss well with the spring onions and herbs until thoroughly combined. Serve immediately.

Rounded flavours, simmered stocks, bubbling curries and saucy stews

Slow, gentle cooking helps to produce deliciously rounded flavours in every one of these mouthwatering soups, curries and simmered dishes. From cleansing broths and Thai curries to Chinese braised pork and Italian-style risotto with an Asian twist, this chapter is full of enticingly inspired dishes to really savour and take your time over. Gentle simmering allows the flavours of the dish to develop. Spices and aromatics mellow, flavours mingle, the sweet intensity of coconut milk and root vegetables has time to grow, and meat, poultry and fish become deliciously tender and juicy. Each one of these recipes is irresistibly comforting, and you'll find it almost impossible to stop at just one serving.

Chinese cabbage, meatball and noodle broth

This wonderfully fragrant combination of spiced meatballs, noodles and vegetables cooked slowly in a richly flavoured broth makes for a very hearty, warming soup. Serve it as a main course on a cold winter evening, drizzled with chilli oil for a little extra heat.

SERVES 4

10 dried shiitake mushrooms

90g/3½oz bean thread noodles

675g/1½lb minced (ground) beef

10ml/2 tsp finely grated garlic

10ml/2 tsp finely grated fresh root ginger

1 red chilli, seeded and chopped

6 spring onions (scallions), finely sliced

1 egg white

15ml/1 tbsp cornflour (cornstarch)

15ml/1 tbsp Chinese rice wine

30ml/2 tbsp sunflower oil

1.5 litres/2½ pints/6¼ cups chicken or beef stock

50ml/2fl oz/¼ cup light soy sauce

5ml/1 tsp sugar

150g/5oz enokitake mushrooms, trimmed

200g/7oz Chinese cabbage, very thinly sliced

salt and ground black pepper

sesame oil and chilli oil, to drizzle (optional)

1 Place the dried mushrooms in a bowl and pour over 250ml/8fl oz/1 cup boiling water. Leave to soak for 30 minutes and then squeeze dry, reserving the soaking liquid.

2 Cut the stems from the mushrooms and discard, then thickly slice the caps and set aside.

3 Put the noodles in a large bowl and pour over boiling water to cover. Leave to soak for 3–4 minutes, then drain, rinse and set aside.

4 Place the beef, garlic, ginger, chilli, spring onions, egg white, cornflour, rice wine and seasoning in a food processor. Process to combine well.

5 Transfer the mixture to a bowl and divide into 30 portions, then shape each one into a ball.

6 Heat a wok over a high heat and add the oil. Fry the meatballs, in batches, for 2–3 minutes on each side until lightly browned. Remove with a slotted spoon and drain on kitchen paper.

7 Wipe out the wok and place over a high heat. Add the stock, soy sauce, sugar and shiitake mushrooms with the reserved soaking liquid and bring to the boil.

8 Add the meatballs to the boiling stock, reduce the heat and cook gently for 20–25 minutes.

9 Add the noodles, enoki mushrooms and cabbage to the wok and cook gently for 4–5 minutes. Serve ladled into wide shallow bowls. Drizzle with sesame oil and chilli oil if liked.

Tofu and bean sprout soup with rice noodles

This light and refreshing soup is very quick and simple to make. The aromatic, spicy broth is simmered first, before adding the tofu, bean sprouts and noodles for very brief cooking. Make sure you use firm tofu because the softer variety will disintegrate during cooking.

SERVES 4

150g/5oz dried thick rice noodles	5ml/1 tsp finely sliced garlic
1 litre/1¾ pints/4 cups vegetable stock	5ml/1 tsp finely chopped fresh root ginger
1 red chilli, seeded and finely sliced	200g/7oz firm tofu, cubed
15ml/1 tbsp light soy sauce	90g/3½oz mung bean sprouts
juice of 1 small lime	30ml/2 tbsp chopped fresh mint
10ml/2 tsp palm sugar	15ml/1 tbsp chopped fresh coriander (cilantro)
	15ml/1 tbsp chopped fresh sweet basil
	50g/2oz roasted peanuts, roughly chopped
	spring onion (scallion) slivers and red (bell) pepper slivers, to garnish

1 Place the noodles in a bowl and pour over enough boiling water to cover. Soak for 10–15 minutes, until soft. Drain, rinse and set aside.

2 Meanwhile, place the stock, red chilli, soy sauce, lime juice, sugar, garlic and ginger in a wok over a high heat. Bring to the boil, cover, reduce to a low heat and simmer gently for 10–12 minutes.

3 Add the drained noodles, tofu and mung bean sprouts and cook gently for 2–3 minutes. Remove from the heat and stir in the chopped herbs.

4 Ladle the soup into bowls and scatter over the peanuts. Garnish with spring onion and red pepper slivers if liked.

Indian-style spiced red lentil and tomato dhal

This is Indian comfort food at its best – there's nothing like a bowl of dhal spiced with mustard seeds, cumin and coriander to clear away the blues. Make sure you serve it with plenty of bread to mop up the delicious juices.

SERVES 4

30ml/2 tbsp sunflower oil

1 green chilli, halved

2 red onions, halved and thinly sliced

10ml/2 tsp finely grated garlic

10ml/2 tsp finely grated fresh root ginger

10ml/2 tsp black mustard seeds

15ml/1 tbsp cumin seeds

10ml/2 tsp crushed coriander seeds

10 curry leaves

250g/9oz/generous 1 cup red lentils

2.5ml/½ tsp turmeric

2 plum tomatoes, roughly chopped

salt

coriander (cilantro) leaves and crispy fried onion, to garnish (optional)

yogurt, poppadums and griddled flatbread or naans, to serve

1 Heat a wok over a medium heat and add the sunflower oil. When hot add the green chilli and onions, stir to combine, lower the heat and cook gently for 10–12 minutes, until softened. Increase the heat slightly and add the garlic, ginger, mustard seeds, cumin seeds, coriander seeds and curry leaves and stir-fry for 2–3 minutes.

2 Rinse the lentils in cold water, drain, then add to the wok with 700ml/ 1 pint 2fl oz/scant 3 cups cold water, the turmeric and tomatoes and season with plenty of salt.

3 Bring the mixture to the boil, cover, reduce the heat and cook very gently for 25–30 minutes, stirring occasionally.

4 Check the seasoning, then garnish with coriander leaves and crispy fried onion, if liked, and serve with yogurt, poppadums and flatbread or naans.

Spiced peas If you prefer, you can use yellow split peas in place of the lentils. Like red lentils, these do not need to be soaked before cooking.

Thai yellow vegetable curry

This hot and spicy curry made with coconut milk has a creamy richness that contrasts wonderfully with the heat of chilli and the bite of lightly cooked vegetables. Yellow curry paste is available in supermarkets and is useful if you're in a hurry, but you will really taste the difference when you make this one using fresh herbs, spices and aromatics.

SERVES 4

30ml/2 tbsp sunflower oil

200ml/7fl oz/scant 1 cup coconut cream

300ml/½ pint/1¼ cups coconut milk

150ml/¼ pint/⅔ cup vegetable stock

200g/7oz snake beans, cut into 2cm/¾in lengths

200g/7oz baby corn

4 baby courgettes (zucchini), sliced

1 small aubergine (eggplant), cubed or sliced

30ml/2 tbsp fish sauce

10ml/2 tsp palm sugar

fresh coriander (cilantro) leaves, to garnish

noodles or rice, to serve

FOR THE CURRY PASTE

10ml/2 tsp hot chilli powder

10ml/2 tsp ground coriander

10ml/2 tsp ground cumin

5ml/1 tsp turmeric

15ml/1 tbsp chopped fresh galangal

10ml/2 tsp finely grated garlic

30ml/2 tbsp finely chopped lemon grass

4 red Asian shallots, finely chopped

5ml/1 tsp shrimp paste

5ml/1 tsp finely chopped lime rind

1 Make the curry paste. Place all the ingredients in a small food processor and blend with 30–45ml/2–3 tbsp of cold water to make a smooth paste. Add a little more water if the paste seems too dry.

2 Heat a large wok over a medium heat and add the sunflower oil. When hot add 30–45ml/2–3 tbsp of the curry paste and stir-fry for 1–2 minutes. Add the coconut cream and cook gently for 8–10 minutes, or until the mixture starts to separate.

3 Add the coconut milk, stock and vegetables and cook gently for 8–10 minutes, until the vegetables are just tender. Stir in the fish sauce and palm sugar, garnish with coriander leaves and serve with noodles or rice.

Making your own curry paste
You will need a good food processor, preferably one with an attachment for blending smaller quantities. Alternatively, you can use a large mortar and pestle, but be warned – it will be hard work. Store any remaining curry paste in a screw-top jar in the refrigerator for up to a week.

Spicy chickpeas with spinach

This richly flavoured dish makes a great main meal for vegetarians, but it will be equally popular with meat-eaters. It is particularly good served drizzled with a little lightly beaten plain yogurt – the sharp, creamy flavour complements the complex spices perfectly.

SERVES 4

200g/7oz dried chickpeas

30ml/2 tbsp sunflower oil

2 onions, halved and thinly sliced

10ml/2 tsp ground coriander

10ml/2 tsp ground cumin

5ml/1 tsp hot chilli powder

2.5ml/½ tsp turmeric

15ml/1 tbsp medium curry powder

400g/14oz can chopped tomatoes

5ml/1 tsp caster (superfine) sugar

salt and ground black pepper

30ml/2 tbsp chopped mint leaves

115g/4oz baby leaf spinach

steamed rice or bread, to serve

1 Soak the chickpeas in cold water overnight. Drain, rinse and place in a large pan. Cover with water and bring to the boil. Reduce the heat and simmer for 45 minutes, or until just tender. Drain and set aside.

2 Heat the oil in a wok, add the onions and cook over a low heat for 15 minutes, until lightly golden. Add the ground coriander and cumin, chilli powder, turmeric and curry powder and stir-fry for 1–2 minutes.

3 Add the tomatoes, sugar and 105ml/7 tbsp water to the wok and bring to the boil. Cover, reduce the heat and simmer gently for 15 minutes.

4 Add the chickpeas to the wok, season well and cook gently for 8–10 minutes. Stir in the chopped mint.

5 Divide the spinach leaves between shallow bowls, top with the chickpea mixture and serve with some steamed rice or bread.

Goan prawn curry with mango and coconut milk

This sweet, spicy, hot-and-sour curry comes from the shores of Western India. It is simple to make, and the addition of mango and tamarind produces a very full, rich flavour. If you have time, make it the day before to give the flavours time to develop. Simply reheat to serve.

SERVES 4

5ml/1 tsp hot chilli powder

15ml/1 tbsp paprika

2.5ml/½ tsp turmeric

4 garlic cloves, crushed

10ml/2 tsp finely grated ginger

30ml/2 tbsp ground coriander

10ml/2 tsp ground cumin

15ml/1 tbsp jaggery or palm sugar

1 green mango, sliced and stoned

400g/14oz can coconut milk

10ml/2 tsp salt

15ml/1 tbsp tamarind paste

1kg/2¼lb large prawns (shrimp), heads and tails on

chopped coriander (cilantro), to garnish

steamed white rice, to serve

chopped tomato, cucumber and onion salad, to serve

1 In a large bowl, combine the chilli powder, paprika, turmeric, garlic, ginger, ground coriander, ground cumin and jaggery or palm sugar.

2 Add 400ml/14fl oz/1⅔ cups cold water to the bowl and stir to combine.

3 Pour the spice mixture into a wok and place over a high heat and bring the mixture to the boil. Cover the wok with a lid, reduce the heat to low and simmer gently for 8–10 minutes.

4 Add the mango, coconut milk, salt and tamarind paste to the wok and stir to combine. Bring to a simmer and then add the prawns.

5 Cover the wok and cook gently for 10–12 minutes, or until the prawns have turned pink and are cooked through.

6 Serve the curry garnished with chopped coriander, accompanied by steamed white rice and a tomato, cucumber and onion salad.

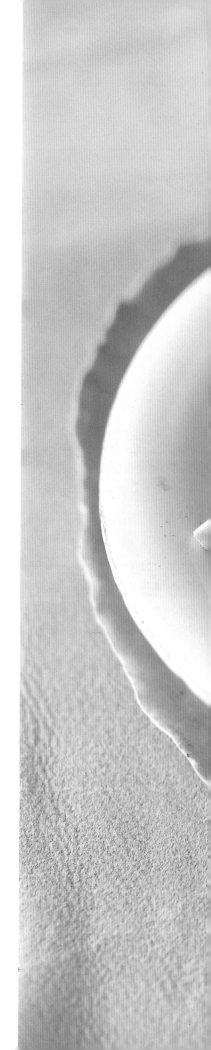

Steamed langoustine with lemon grass risotto

Traditional Italian risotto is given a subtle Asian twist with the addition of fragrant lemon grass, Asian fish sauce and Chinese chives. The delicate citrus-flavoured rice is the perfect accompaniment to simply steamed langoustines. If you can't find fresh langoustines (also known as Dublin Bay prawns) you can use king prawns in their shells instead.

SERVES 4

8 fresh langoustines

30ml/2 tbsp olive oil

15ml/1 tbsp butter

1 onion, finely chopped

1 carrot, finely diced

1 celery stick, finely diced

30ml/2 tbsp very finely chopped lemon grass

300g/11oz/1½ cups arborio rice

200ml/7fl oz/scant 1 cup dry white wine

1.5 litres/2½ pints/6¼ cups boiling vegetable stock

50ml/2fl oz/¼ cup fish sauce

30ml/2 tbsp finely chopped Chinese chives

salt and ground black pepper

1 Place the langoustines in a baking parchment-lined bamboo steamer, cover and place over a wok of simmering water. Steam for 6–8 minutes, remove from the heat and keep warm.

2 Heat the oil and butter in a wok and add the vegetables. Cook over a high heat for 2–3 minutes. Add the lemon grass and rice and stir-fry for 2 minutes.

3 Add the wine to the wok, reduce the heat and slowly stir until the wine is absorbed. Add about 250ml/8fl oz/ 1 cup of the stock and cook gently, stirring until absorbed. Continue adding the stock, about 120ml/4fl oz/ ½ cup at a time, stirring until fully absorbed before adding more. Cook until the rice is just tender.

4 Stir the fish sauce and the Chinese chives into the risotto, check the seasoning and serve on warmed plates. Top each serving with 2 langoustines.

Spiced halibut and tomato curry

The chunky cubes of white fish contrast beautifully with the rich red spicy tomato sauce and taste just as good as they look. Halibut is used here, but you can use any type of firm white fish for this recipe.

SERVES 4

60ml/4 tbsp lemon juice

60ml/4 tbsp rice wine vinegar

30ml/2 tbsp cumin seeds

5ml/1 tsp turmeric

5ml/1 tsp chilli powder

5ml/1 tsp salt

750g/1lb 11oz thick halibut fillets, skinned and cubed

60ml/4 tbsp sunflower oil

1 onion, finely chopped

3 garlic cloves, finely grated

30ml/2 tbsp finely grated fresh root ginger

10ml/2 tsp black mustard seeds

2 x 400g/14oz cans chopped tomatoes

5ml/1 tsp sugar

chopped coriander (cilantro) and sliced green chilli, to garnish

natural (plain) yogurt, to drizzle (optional)

basmati rice, pickles and poppadums, to serve

1 Mix together the lemon juice, vinegar, cumin, turmeric, chilli powder and salt in a shallow glass bowl. Add the cubed fish and turn to coat evenly. Cover and put in the refrigerator to marinate for 25–30 minutes.

2 Meanwhile, heat a wok over a high heat and add the oil. When hot, add the onion, garlic, ginger and mustard seeds. Reduce the heat to low and cook very gently for about 10 minutes, stirring occasionally.

3 Add the tomatoes and sugar to the wok, bring to a boil, reduce the heat, cover and cook gently for 15–20 minutes, stirring occasionally.

4 Add the fish and its marinade to the wok, stir gently to mix, then cover and simmer gently for 15–20 minutes, or until the fish is cooked through and flakes easily with a fork.

5 Serve the curry ladled into shallow bowls with basmati rice, pickles and poppadums. Garnish with fresh coriander and green chillies, and drizzle over some natural yogurt if liked.

Fragrant tarragon chicken with garlic and pickled lemons

Chicken thighs have a particularly good flavour and stand up well to the robust ingredients used in this dish. Pickled lemons, also known as preserved lemons, are a popular flavouring in North African and Middle Eastern cooking. They are widely available in most large supermarkets and give this dish a wonderfully zesty, fragrant flavour.

SERVES 4

3 heads of garlic, separated but still in their skins

2 onions, quartered

8 chicken thighs

90ml/6 tbsp chopped fresh tarragon leaves

8 small pickled lemons, roughly chopped

30–45ml/2–3 tbsp olive oil

750ml/1¼ pints/3 cups dessert wine

250ml/8fl oz/1 cup chicken stock

sea salt and ground black pepper

sautéed potatoes and steamed yellow or green beans, to serve

1 Arrange the garlic and quartered onions in the base of a large wok and lay the chicken thighs over the top in a single layer.

2 Sprinkle the tarragon and chopped pickled lemons over the top of the chicken, season well with salt and ground black pepper and drizzle over the olive oil.

3 Pour the wine and stock over the chicken and bring to the boil. Cover the wok tightly, reduce the heat to low and simmer gently for 1½ hours.

4 Remove the wok from the heat, and leave to stand, covered, for 10 minutes before serving with sautéed potatoes and steamed yellow or green beans.

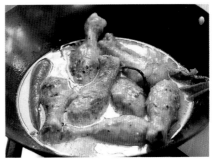

Spiced coconut chicken with cardamom, chilli and ginger

You need to plan ahead to make this luxurious chicken curry. The chicken legs are marinated overnight in an aromatic blend of yogurt and spices before being gently simmered with hot green chillies in creamy coconut milk. Serve with rice or Indian breads.

SERVES 4

1.6kg/3½lb large chicken drumsticks

30ml/2 tbsp sunflower oil

400ml/14fl oz/1⅔ cups coconut milk

4–6 large green chillies, halved

45ml/3 tbsp finely chopped coriander (cilantro)

salt and ground black pepper

natural yogurt, to drizzle

FOR THE MARINADE

15ml/1 tbsp crushed cardamom seeds

15ml/1 tbsp grated fresh root ginger

10ml/2 tsp finely grated garlic

105ml/7 tbsp natural (plain) yogurt

2 green chillies, seeded and chopped

5ml/1 tsp ground cumin

5ml/1 tsp ground coriander

5ml/1 tsp turmeric

finely grated zest and juice of 1 lime

1 Make the marinade. Place the cardamom, ginger, garlic, half the yogurt, green chillies, cumin, coriander, turmeric and lime zest and juice in a blender. Process until smooth, season and pour into a large glass bowl.

2 Add the chicken to the marinade and toss to coat evenly. Cover the bowl and marinate in the refrigerator for 6–8 hours, or overnight if time permits.

3 Heat the oil in a large, non-stick wok over a low heat. Remove the chicken from the marinade, reserving the marinade. Add the chicken to the wok and brown all over, then add the coconut milk, remaining yogurt, reserved marinade and green chillies and bring to a boil.

4 Reduce the heat and simmer gently, uncovered for 30–35 minutes. Check the seasoning, adding more if needed. Stir in the coriander, ladle into warmed bowls and serve immediately. Drizzle with yogurt if liked.

Thai-style red duck curry with pea aubergines

The rich flavour of duck is perfectly suited to this red hot curry. Tiny pea aubergines are available in Asian stores, but if you have difficulty finding them, use larger aubergines cut into bitesize chunks.

SERVES 4

4 duck breast portions

400ml/14fl oz can coconut milk

200ml/7fl oz/scant 1 cup chicken stock

30ml/2 tbsp red Thai curry paste

8 spring onions (scallions), finely sliced

10ml/2 tsp grated fresh root ginger

30ml/2 tbsp Chinese rice wine

15ml/1 tbsp fish sauce

15ml/1 tbsp soy sauce

2 lemon grass stalks, halved lengthways

3–4 kaffir lime leaves

300g/11oz pea aubergines (eggplants)

10ml/2 tsp sugar

salt and ground black pepper

10–12 fresh basil and mint leaves, to garnish

steamed jasmine rice, to serve

1 Using a sharp knife, cut the duck breast portions into bitesize pieces.

2 Place a wok over a low heat and add the coconut milk, stock, curry paste, spring onions, ginger, rice wine, fish and soy sauces, lemon grass and lime leaves. Slowly bring to the boil.

3 Add the duck, aubergines and sugar to the wok and gently simmer for 25–30 minutes, stirring occasionally.

4 Remove the wok from the heat and leave to stand, covered, for about 15 minutes. Season to taste and serve ladled into shallow bowls with steamed jasmine rice, garnished with fresh mint and basil leaves.

Chinese braised pork belly with Asian greens

Pork belly becomes meltingly tender in this slow-braised dish flavoured with orange, cinnamon, star anise and ginger. The flavours meld and mellow during cooking to produce a rich, complex rounded taste. Serve simply with plain rice and steamed Asian greens.

SERVES 4

800g/1¾lb pork belly, trimmed and cut into 12 pieces

400ml/14fl oz/1⅔ cups beef stock

75ml/5 tbsp soy sauce

finely grated zest and juice of 1 large orange

15ml/1 tbsp finely shredded fresh root ginger

2 garlic cloves, sliced

15ml/1 tbsp hot chilli powder

15ml/1 tbsp dark muscovado (molasses) sugar

3 cinnamon sticks

3 cloves

10 black peppercorns

2–3 star anise

steamed greens and rice, to serve

1 Place the pork in a wok and pour over water to cover. Bring the water to the boil. Cover, reduce the heat and cook gently for 30 minutes. Drain the pork and return to the wok with the stock, soy sauce, orange zest and juice, ginger, garlic, chilli powder, muscovado sugar, cinnamon sticks, cloves, peppercorns and star anise.

2 Pour over water to just cover the pork belly pieces and cook on a high heat until the mixture comes to a boil.

3 Cover the wok tightly with a lid, then reduce the heat to low and cook gently for 1½ hours, stirring occasionally. (Check the pork occasionally during cooking to ensure it doesn't stick to the base of the wok.)

4 Uncover the wok and simmer for 30 minutes, stirring occasionally until the meat is very tender. Serve with steamed greens and rice.

Choosing greens Any type of Asian greens will go well with this dish. Try pak choi (bok choy), choi sum or Chinese broccoli.

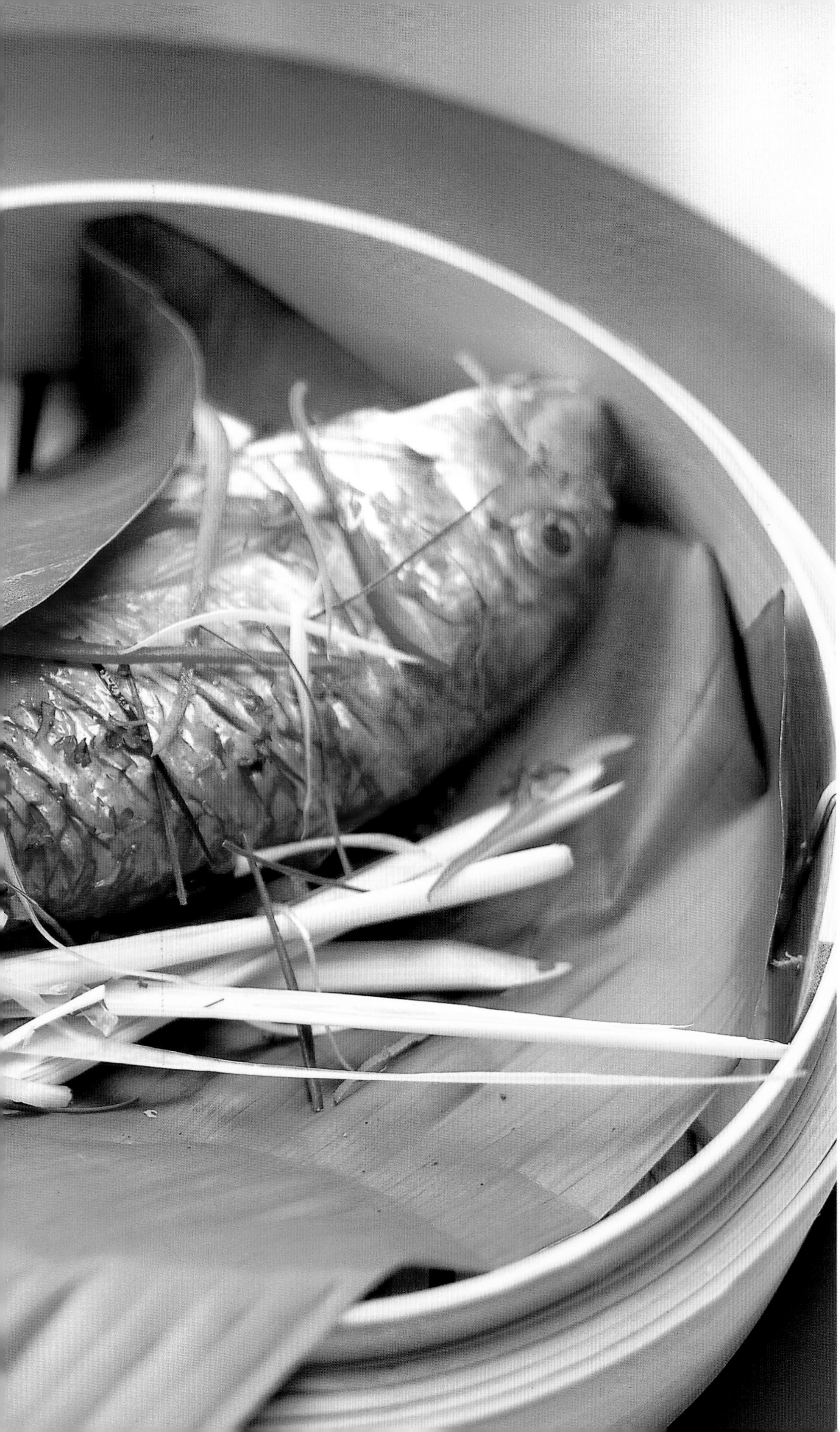

Hot and steamy

Moist heat, succulent textures, delicate flavours and spicy marinades

There's something utterly delicious about food cooked in hot, moist steam – whether it's prawns wrapped tightly in parchment paper and steamed in their own juices, or fresh vegetables delicately steamed over simmering water, then tossed with noodles and aromatic flavourings. The food seems to take on a wonderful moistness and melt-in-the mouth quality, and the subtlety of this delicate cooking method seems to come through in both the taste and texture. The dishes in this chapter make perfect use of the natural flavours of the ingredients, enhancing them with the addition of fresh herbs, spices and aromatics. Delicate tofu, poultry and fish are enlivened with wonderfully fragrant marinades, while dishes such as herb, chilli and pandanus steamed fish custards and deliciously doughy Chinese steamed pork buns hold their own surprises.

Herb and chilli aubergines

Plump and juicy aubergines are delicious steamed until tender and then tossed in a fragrant minty dressing with crunchy water chestnuts. The combination of textures and flavours is absolutely sensational.

SERVES 4

500g/1¼lb firm, baby aubergines (eggplants)

30ml/2 tbsp sunflower oil

6 garlic cloves, very finely chopped

15ml/1 tbsp very finely chopped fresh root ginger

8 spring onions (scallions), cut diagonally into 2.5cm/1in lengths

2 red chillies, seeded and thinly sliced

45ml/3 tbsp light soy sauce

15ml/1 tbsp Chinese rice wine

15ml/1 tbsp golden caster (superfine) sugar or palm sugar

a large handful of mint leaves

30–45ml/2–3 tbsp roughly chopped coriander (cilantro) leaves

115g/4oz water chestnuts

50g/2oz roasted peanuts, roughly chopped

steamed egg noodles or rice, to serve

1 Cut the aubergines in half lengthways and place on a heatproof plate.

2 Place a steamer rack in a wok and add 5cm/2in of water. Bring the water to the boil and lower the plate on to the rack and reduce the heat to low. Cover and steam the aubergines for 25–30 minutes, until they are cooked through. (Check the water level regularly, adding more if necessary.) Set aside the aubergines to cool.

3 Place the oil in a clean, dry wok and place over a medium heat. When hot, add the garlic, ginger, spring onions and chillies and stir-fry for 2–3 minutes. Remove from the heat and stir in the soy sauce, rice wine and sugar.

4 Add the mint leaves, chopped coriander, water chestnuts and peanuts to the aubergine and toss. Pour the garlic-ginger mixture evenly over the vegetables, toss gently and serve with steamed egg noodles or rice.

Vegetable noodles with yellow bean sauce

Yellow bean sauce adds a distinctive Chinese flavour to this wonderfully simple dish of spicy vegetables and noodles. The sauce is made from fermented yellow beans and has a marvellous texture and spicy, aromatic flavour. However, be very careful not too add too much, because it is very salty – and if you overdo it, the final flavour of the dish will be spoiled.

SERVES 4

150g/5oz thin egg noodles

200g/7oz baby leeks, sliced lengthways

200g/7oz baby courgettes (zucchini), halved lengthways

200g/7oz sugarsnap peas, trimmed

200g/7oz peas

15ml/1 tbsp sunflower oil

5 garlic cloves, sliced

45ml/3 tbsp yellow bean sauce

45ml/3 tbsp sweet chilli sauce

30ml/2 tbsp sweet soy sauce

cashew nuts, to garnish

1 Cook the noodles according to the packet instructions, drain and set aside.

2 Line a large bamboo steamer with perforated baking parchment and place the leeks, courgettes and both types of peas in it. Cover and suspend the steamer over a wok of simmering water. Steam the vegetables for about 5 minutes, then remove and set aside.

3 Pour the water from the wok and wipe dry with kitchen paper. Pour the sunflower oil into the wok and place over a medium heat. Add the sliced garlic and stir-fry for 1–2 minutes.

4 In a separate bowl, mix together the yellow bean, sweet chilli and soy sauces, then pour into the wok. Stir to mix with the garlic, then add the steamed vegetables and the noodles and toss together to combine.

5 Cook the vegetables and noodles for 2–3 minutes, stirring frequently, until heated through.

6 To serve, divide the vegetable noodles among four warmed serving bowls and and scatter over the cashew nuts to garnish.

Marinated tofu and broccoli with crispy fried shallots

This meltingly tender tofu flavoured with a fragrant blend of spices and served with tender young stems of broccoli makes a perfect light supper or lunch. You can buy the crispy fried shallots from Asian supermarkets, but they are very easy to make yourself.

SERVES 4

500g/1¼lb block of firm tofu, drained

45ml/3 tbsp kecap manis

30ml/2 tbsp sweet chilli sauce

45ml/3 tbsp soy sauce

5ml/1 tsp sesame oil

5ml/1 tsp finely grated fresh root ginger

400g/14oz tenderstem broccoli, halved lengthways

45ml/3 tbsp roughly chopped coriander (cilantro)

30ml/2 tbsp toasted sesame seeds

30ml/2 tbsp crispy fried shallots

steamed white rice or noodles, to serve

1 Cut the tofu into 4 triangular pieces: slice the block in half widthways, then diagonally. Place in a heatproof dish.

2 In a small bowl, combine the kecap manis, chilli sauce, soy sauce, sesame oil and ginger, then pour over the tofu. Leave the tofu to marinate for at least 30 minutes, turning occasionally.

3 Place the broccoli on a heatproof plate and place on a trivet or steamer rack in the wok. Cover and steam for 4–5 minutes, until just tender. Remove and keep warm.

4 Place the dish of tofu on the trivet or steamer rack in the wok, cover and steam for 4–5 minutes.

5 Divide the broccolli among four warmed serving plates and top each one with a piece of tofu.

6 Spoon the remaining juices over the tofu and broccolli, then sprinkle over the coriander, sesame seeds and crispy shallots. Serve immediately with steamed white rice or noodles.

Steamed scallops with ginger, spring onion and chives

Serve these juicy, fragrant scallops with their subtly spiced flavour as an indulgent main course for a special occasion. For the best results, use the freshest scallops you can find, and if you're worried about shucking them yourself, ask your fishmonger to do it for you.

SERVES 4

24 king scallops in their shells, cleaned

15ml/1 tbsp very finely shredded fresh root ginger

5ml/1 tsp very finely chopped garlic

1 large red chilli, seeded and very finely chopped

15ml/1 tbsp light soy sauce

15ml/1 tbsp Chinese rice wine

a few drops of sesame oil

2–3 spring onions (scallions), very finely shredded

15ml/1 tbsp very finely chopped fresh chives

noodles or rice, to serve

1 Remove the scallops from their shells, then remove the membrane and hard white muscle from each one. Arrrange the scallops on two plates. Rinse the shells, dry and set aside.

2 Fill two woks with 5cm/2in water and place a trivet in the base of each one. Bring to the boil.

3 Meanwhile, mix together the ginger, garlic, chilli, soy sauce, rice wine, sesame oil, spring onions and chives and spoon over the scallops.

4 Lower a plate of scallops into each of the woks. Turn the heat to low, cover and steam for 10–12 minutes, or until just cooked through.

5 Divide the scallops among four, or eight, of the reserved shells and serve immediately with noodles or rice.

Lemon, chilli and herb steamed razor clams

Razor clams have beautiful striped gold and brown tubular shells and make a wonderful appetizer for a special meal. Here they are lightly steamed and tossed in a fragrant, Italian-style dressing of chilli, lemon, garlic and parsley. It really is a marriage made in heaven! Serve with crusty bread for mopping up the juices. To serve as a main course, simply double the quantity.

SERVES 4

12 razor clams

90–120ml/6–8 tbsp extra virgin olive oil

finely grated rind and juice of 1 small lemon

2 garlic cloves, very finely grated

1 red chilli, seeded and very finely chopped

60ml/4 tbsp chopped flat leaf parsley

salt and ground black pepper

mixed salad leaves and crusty bread, to serve

1 Wash the razor clams well in plenty of cold running water. Drain and arrange half the clams in a steamer, with the hinge-side down.

2 Pour 5cm/2in water into a wok and bring to the boil. Carefully balance the steamer over the water and cover tightly. Steam for 3–4 minutes, or until the clams have fully opened. Carefully remove the clams from the wok and keep warm while you steam the remaining clams in the same way.

3 In a bowl, mix together the olive oil, grated lemon rind and juice, garlic, red chilli and flat leaf parsley. Season well with salt and pepper. Spoon the mixture over the steamed clams and serve immediately with a crisp mixed-leaf salad and crusty bread.

If you can't find razorshell clams
You can use venus clams or mussels in place of the razor shells if you prefer. You will need about 1kg/2¼lb. Clean the clams or mussels well, scraping off the beard from the mussels. Discard any open clams or mussels that do not close when tapped with the back of a knife. After steaming, discard any that remain closed.

Parchment-wrapped prawns

These succulent pink prawns coated in a fragrant spice paste make the perfect dish for informal entertaining. Serve the prawns in their paper parcels and allow your guests to unwrap them at the table and enjoy the heady aroma of Thai spices as each packet is opened.

SERVES 4

2 lemon grass stalks, very finely chopped

5ml/1 tsp very finely chopped galangal

4 garlic cloves, finely chopped

finely grated rind and juice of 1 lime

4 spring onions (scallions), chopped

10ml/2 tsp palm sugar

15ml/1 tbsp soy sauce

5ml/1 tsp fish sauce

5ml/1 tsp chilli oil

45ml/3 tbsp chopped fresh coriander (cilantro) leaves

30ml/2 tbsp chopped fresh Thai basil leaves

1kg/2¼lb raw tiger prawns (shrimp), peeled and deveined with tails left on

basil leaves and lime wedges, to garnish

1 Place the lemon grass, galangal, garlic, lime rind and juice and spring onions in a food processor. Blend in short bursts until the mixture forms a coarse paste.

2 Transfer the paste to a large bowl and stir in the palm sugar, soy sauce, fish sauce, chilli oil and chopped herbs.

3 Add the prawns to the paste and toss to coat evenly. Cover and marinate in the refrigerator for 30 minutes–1 hour.

4 Cut out eight 20cm/8in squares of baking parchment. Place one-eighth of the prawn mixture in the centre of each one, then fold over the edges and twist together to make a sealed parcel.

5 Place the parcels in a large bamboo steamer, cover and steam over a wok of simmering water for 10 minutes, or until the prawns are just cooked through. Serve immediately garnished with basil leaves and lime wedges.

Herb, chilli and pandanus steamed fish custards

These pretty little custards make an unusual and exotic appetizer for a dinner party. The pandanus leaves impart a distinctive flavour – but don't be tempted to eat them once the custards are cooked!

SERVES 4

2 eggs

200ml/7fl oz/scant 1 cup coconut cream

60ml/4 tbsp chopped fresh coriander (cilantro)

1 red chilli, seeded and sliced

15ml/1 tbsp finely chopped lemon grass

2 kaffir lime leaves, finely shredded

30ml/2 tbsp red Thai curry paste

1 garlic clove, crushed

5ml/1 tsp finely grated ginger

2 spring onions (scallions), finely sliced

300g/11oz mixed firm white fish fillets (cod, halibut or haddock), skinned

200g/7oz raw tiger prawns (shrimp), peeled and deveined

4-6 pandanus leaves

salt and ground black pepper

shredded cucumber, steamed rice and soy sauce, to serve

1 Beat the eggs in a bowl, then stir in the coconut cream, coriander, chilli, lemon grass, lime leaves, curry paste, garlic, ginger and spring onions. Finely chop the fish and roughly chop the prawns and add to the egg mixture. Stir well and season.

2 Grease 4 ramekins and line them with the pandanus leaves. Divide the fish mixture between them, then arrange in a bamboo steamer.

3 Pour 5cm/2in water into a wok and bring to the boil. Suspend the steamer over the water, cover, reduce the heat to low and steam for 25–30 minutes, or until the fish is cooked through. Serve immediately with shredded cucumber, steamed rice and soy sauce.

Fragrant red snapper in banana leaves

Shiny, dark green banana leaves make a really good wrapping for steamed fish. Here, whole red snappers are wrapped with a fragrant mix of coconut cream, mint, coriander, kaffir lime leaves, lemon grass and chilli to make an impressive main course.

SERVES 4

4 small red snapper, grouper, tilapia or red bream, gutted and cleaned

4 large squares of banana leaf (approximately 30cm/12in square)

50ml/2fl oz/¼ cup coconut cream

90ml/6 tbsp chopped coriander (cilantro)

90ml/6 tbsp chopped mint

juice of 3 limes

3 spring onions (scallions), finely sliced

4 kaffir lime leaves, finely shredded

2 red chillies, seeded and finely sliced

4 lemon grass stalks, split lengthways

salt and ground black pepper

steamed rice and steamed Asian greens, to serve

1 Using a small sharp knife, score the fish diagonally on each side.

2 Bring a wok of water to the boil and dip each square of banana leaf into it for 15–20 seconds. Rinse under cold water and dry with kitchen paper.

3 Place the coconut cream, chopped herbs, lime juice, spring onions, lime leaves and chillies in a bowl and stir well to mix. Season with salt and pepper.

4 Lay each banana leaf out flat on a work surface and place a fish and a split lemon grass stalk in the centre of each one. Spread the herb mixture over each fish.

5 Wrap the banana leaf around each one to form four neat parcels. Secure each parcel tightly with a bamboo skewer or a cocktail stick (toothpick).

6 Place the parcels in a single layer in one or two tiers of a large bamboo steamer and place over a wok of simmering water. Cover tightly and steam for 15–20 minutes, or until the fish is cooked through.

7 Remove the fish from the steamer and serve immediately, still in their banana-leaf wrappings, with steamed rice and steamed Asian greens.

Mackerel with shiitake mushrooms and black beans

Earthy-tasting shiitake mushrooms, zesty fresh ginger and pungent salted black beans are the perfect partners for robustly flavoured mackerel fillets. The striking combination of flavours all come together beautifully, complementing, rather than overwhelming, each other.

SERVES 4

8 x 115g/4oz mackerel fillets

20 dried shiitake mushrooms

15ml/1 tbsp finely julienned fresh root ginger

3 star anise

45ml/3 tbsp dark soy sauce

15ml/1 tbsp Chinese rice wine

15ml/1 tbsp salted black beans

6 spring onions (scallions), finely shredded

30ml/2 tbsp sunflower oil

5ml/1 tsp sesame oil

4 garlic cloves, very thinly sliced

sliced cucumber and steamed basmati rice, to serve

1 Divide the mackerel fillets between two lightly oiled heatproof plates, with the skin-side up. Using a a small, sharp knife, make 3–4 diagonal slits in each one, then set aside.

2 Place the dried shiitake mushrooms in a large bowl and pour over enough boiling water to cover. Leave to soak for 20–25 minutes. Drain, reserving the soaking liquid, discard the stems and slice the caps thinly.

3 Place a trivet or a steamer rack in a large wok and pour in 5cm/2in of the mushroom liquid (top up with water if necessary). Add half the ginger and the star anise.

4 Push the remaining ginger strips into the slits in the fish and scatter over the sliced mushrooms. Bring the liquid in the wok to a boil and lower one of the prepared plates on to the trivet. Cover the wok, reduce the heat and steam for 10–12 minutes, or until the mackerel is cooked through. Remove the plate from the wok and repeat with the second plate of fish, replenishing the liquid in the wok if necessary.

5 Transfer the steamed fish to a large serving platter. Ladle 105ml/7 tbsp of the steaming liquid into a clean wok with the soy sauce, wine and black beans, place over a gentle heat and bring to a simmer. Spoon over the fish and sprinkle over the spring onions.

6 Wipe out the wok with a piece of kitchen paper and place the wok over a medium heat. Add the oils and garlic and stir-fry for a few minutes until lightly golden. Pour over the fish and serve immediately with sliced cucumber and steamed basmati rice.

Lotus leaf parcels filled with chicken, rice and vegetables

The lotus leaves impart a delicious smoky flavour to the sticky jasmine rice in this dish, which makes a great lunch or supper. You can buy the dried leaves from Asian supermarkets but be sure to choose a packet in which they are fairly intact because they crumble easily.

SERVES 4

2 large lotus leaves

300g/11oz/1½ cups Thai jasmine rice

400ml/14fl oz/1⅔ cups vegetable or chicken stock

8 dried shiitake mushrooms

15ml/1 tbsp sunflower oil

200g/7oz chicken thigh fillets, cut into small cubes

50g/2oz pancetta, cubed

3 garlic cloves, finely sliced

10ml/2 tsp finely grated fresh root ginger

50g/2oz carrots, cut into thin batons

50g/2oz mangetout (snow peas), halved lengthways

60ml/4 tbsp light soy sauce

15ml/1 tbsp Chinese rice wine

5ml/1 tsp cornflour (cornstarch)

1 Place the lotus leaves in a large bowl and pour over enough hot water to cover. Leave to soak for 1½ hours. Drain and cut in half, then set aside.

2 Place the rice in a wok and pour over the stock. Bring to the boil, then reduce the heat, cover and cook gently for 10 minutes. Remove from the heat and leave to stand.

3 Meanwhile soak the mushrooms in boiling water for 15 minutes, then drain, reserving the soaking liquid. Squeeze the mushrooms dry, discard the stems and thinly slice the caps. Set aside.

4 Add the oil to a clean wok and place over a high heat. Add the chicken and pancetta and stir-fry for 2–3 minutes, until lightly browned. Add the garlic, ginger, carrots, mangetout and mushrooms and stir-fry for 30 seconds.

5 Add half the soy sauce, the rice wine and 60ml/4 tbsp of the reserved mushroom liquid to the wok. Combine the cornflour with 15ml/1 tbsp cold water, add to the wok and cook for a few minutes until the mixture thickens. Add the rice and the remaining soy sauce and mix well.

6 Place the lotus leaves on a clean worksurface (brown-side down) and divide the chicken mixture among them. Fold in the sides of the leaves, then roll up and place the parcels, seam-side down, in a baking parchment-lined bamboo steamer.

7 Cover the steamer and place over a wok of simmering water for about 20 minutes (replenishing the water in the wok if necessary). Serve the parcels immediately and unwrap at the table.

Honey, orange and ginger glazed steamed poussins

These moist, succulent poussins coated in a spiced citrus and honey glaze make a great alternative to a traditional roast. Be sure to plan ahead because they need to be marinated for at least 6 hours.

SERVES 4

4 poussins, 300–350g/11–12oz each

juice and finely grated rind of 2 oranges

2 garlic cloves, crushed

15ml/1 tbsp grated fresh root ginger

90ml/6 tbsp soy sauce

75ml/5 tbsp clear honey

2–3 star anise

30ml/2 tbsp Chinese rice wine

about 20 kaffir lime leaves

a large bunch of spring onions (scallions), shredded

60ml/4 tbsp butter

1 large orange, segmented

1 Place the poussins in a deep, non-metallic dish. Combine the orange rind and juice, garlic, ginger, half the soy sauce, half the honey, star anise and rice wine, then pour over the poussins. Turn to coat. Cover and marinate in the refrigerator for at least 6 hours.

2 To cook the poussins, line a large, heatproof plate with the kaffir lime leaves and spring onions. Place the marinated poussins on top and reserve the marinade.

3 Place a trivet or steamer rack in the base of a large wok and pour in 5cm/2in water. Bring to the boil and carefully lower the plate of poussins on to the trivet or rack. Cover, reduce the heat to low and steam for 45 minutes–1 hour, or until the poussins are cooked through and tender. (Check the water level regularly and add more when necessary.)

4 Remove the poussins from the wok and keep warm while you make the glaze. Wipe out the wok and pour in the reserved marinade, butter and the remaining soy sauce and honey. Bring to the boil, reduce the heat and cook gently for 10–15 minutes, or until thick.

5 Spoon the glaze over the poussins and serve immediately, garnished with the orange segments.

Shredded duck and bean thread noodle salad

This refreshing, piquant salad makes a mouthwatering first course or light meal. The rich flavour of duck is offset by the addition of fresh, raw vegetables and zesty dressing. If you prefer, you can use shredded chicken in place of the duck.

SERVES 4

4 duck breast portions

30ml/2 tbsp Chinese rice wine

10ml/2 tsp finely grated fresh root ginger

60ml/4 tbsp soy sauce

15ml/1 tbsp sesame oil

15ml/1 tbsp clear honey

10ml/2 tsp Chinese five-spice powder

toasted sesame seeds, to sprinkle

FOR THE NOODLES

150g/5oz bean-thread noodles

a small handful of fresh mint leaves

a small handful of coriander (cilantro) leaves

1 red (bell) pepper, seeded and finely sliced

4 spring onions (scallions), finely shredded or sliced

50g/2oz mixed salad leaves

FOR THE DRESSING

45ml/3 tbsp light soy sauce

30ml/2 tbsp mirin

10ml/2 tsp golden caster (superfine) sugar

1 garlic clove, crushed

10ml/2 tsp chilli oil

1 Place the duck breast portions in a non-metallic bowl. Mix together the rice wine, ginger, soy sauce, sesame oil, clear honey and five-spice powder. Toss to coat, cover and marinate in the refrigerator for 3–4 hours.

2 Place a large sheet of double thickness of foil on a heatproof plate and place the duck breast portions and marinade on top. Fold the foil to enclose the duck and juices and scrunch the edges to seal.

3 Place a trivet or steamer rack in a large wok and pour in 5cm/2in water. Bring to the boil and carefully lower the plate on to it. Cover tightly, reduce the heat and steam for 50–60 minutes. Remove from the wok and leave to rest for 15 minutes.

4 Meanwhile, place the noodles in a large bowl and pour over enough boiling water to cover. Cover and soak for 5–6 minutes. Drain, refresh under cold water and drain again. Transfer to a large bowl with the herbs, red pepper, spring onions and salad leaves.

5 Mix together all the dressing ingredients. Remove the skin from the duck breasts and roughly shred the flesh using a fork. Divide the noodle salad among four plates and top with the shredded duck. Spoon over the dressing, sprinkle with the sesame seeds and serve immediately.

Steamed pork buns

These deliciously light stuffed buns are a popular street snack sold throughout China. The soft texture of the bun contrasts wonderfully with the spiced meat filling inside. They make an unusual alternative to rice and, once cooked, can be reheated in the steamer.

SERVES 4

30ml/2 tbsp golden caster (superfine) sugar

10ml/2 tsp dried yeast

300g/11oz/2¾ cups plain (all-purpose) flour

30ml/2 tbsp sunflower oil

10ml/2 tsp baking powder

FOR THE FILLING

250g/9oz pork sausages

15ml/1 tbsp barbecue sauce

30ml/2 tbsp oyster sauce

15ml/1 tbsp sweet chilli sauce

15ml/1 tbsp Chinese rice wine

15ml/1 tbsp hoisin sauce

5ml/1 tsp chilli oil

1 To make the dough pour 250ml/ 8fl oz/1 cup warm water into a mixing bowl. Add the sugar and stir to dissolve. Stir in the yeast, cover and leave in a warm place for 15 minutes.

2 Sift the flour into a large mixing bowl and make a well in the centre. Add the sugar and yeast mixture to it with the sunflower oil. Fold the mixture together using your fingers and turn out on to a lightly floured surface.

3 Knead the dough for 8–10 minutes until smooth and elastic. Place in a lightly oiled bowl, cover with a dishtowel and leave to rise in a warm place for 3–4 hours.

4 When risen, place the dough on a lightly floured surface, punch down and shape into a large circle. Sprinkle the baking powder in the centre, bring all the edges towards the centre and knead for 6–8 minutes. Divide the dough into 12 balls, cover with a clean, damp dishtowel and set aside.

5 Squeeze the sausage meat from the casings into a large bowl and stir in the barbecue sauce, oyster sauce, sweet chilli sauce, rice wine, hoisin sauce and chilli oil. Mix thoroughly, using your fingers to combine.

6 Press each dough ball to form a round, 12cm/4½in in diameter. Place a large spoonful of the pork mixture in the centre of each round and bring the edges up to the centre, press together to seal and form a bun shape.

7 Arrange the buns on several layers of a large bamboo steamer, cover and steam over a wok of simmering water for 20–25 minutes, or until they are puffed up and the pork is cooked through. Serve immediately.

Crisp and golden

Sizzling oil, indulgent delicacies, crispy batters and crunchy coatings

There is something decidedly indulgent about deep-fried food – it's hard to tell whether this is because of the wonderful smell, the glorious colour, the combination of crisp and succulent textures or the utterly irresistible taste. This chapter is full of the most wonderful deep-fried dishes, from hot and crispy snacks to light and refreshing salads and divine main meals. Crispy deep-fried noodles will snap between your teeth and melt in your mouth, while golden rice paper parcels and spring rolls will crunch enticingly as you bite into them. Every batter is light as air and every coating is flavoured with aromatic herbs and spices that complement perfectly the glorious tender filling inside.

Asian-style courgette tempura

This is a twist on the classic Japanese tempura, using besan in the batter. Also known as gram flour, golden besan is more commonly used in Indian cooking and gives a wonderfully crisp texture while the courgette inside becomes meltingly tender.

SERVES 4

600g/1lb 5oz courgettes (zucchini)

90g/3½oz/¾ cup besan (chickpea flour)

5ml/1 tsp baking powder

2.5ml/½ tsp turmeric

10ml/2 tsp ground coriander

5ml/1 tsp ground cumin

5ml/1 tsp chilli powder

250ml/8fl oz/1 cup beer

sunflower oil, for frying

salt

steamed basmati rice, natural (plain) yogurt and pickles, to serve

1 Cut the courgettes into thick, finger-sized batons and set aside.

2 Sift the besan, baking powder, turmeric, ground coriander, cumin and chilli powder into a large bowl.

3 Season the mixture with salt and gradually add the beer, mixing to make a thick batter – do not overmix.

4 Fill a large wok, one-third full with sunflower oil and heat to 180°C/350°F (or until a cube of bread, dropped into the oil, browns in 15 seconds).

5 Working in batches, dip the courgette batons in the spiced batter and then deep fry for 1–2 minutes, or until crisp and golden. Lift out of the wok using a slotted spoon and drain on kitchen paper.

6 Serve the courgettes immediately with steamed basmati rice, yogurt, pickles and chutney.

Vegetable tempura You can cook all kinds of vegetables in this way. Try using onion rings, aubergine (eggplant) slices, or even whole mild chillies.

Light and crispy seven-spice aubergines

Thai seven spice powder is a commercial blend of spices, including coriander, cumin, cinnamon, star anise, chilli, cloves and lemon peel. It gives these aubergines a lovely warm flavour that goes very well with the light, curry batter made of whisked egg whites. If you are unable to find it, you can use Chinese five-spice powder instead.

SERVES 4

500g/1¼lb aubergines (eggplant)

15ml/1 tbsp sea salt

2 egg whites

90ml/6 tbsp cornflour (cornstarch)

5ml/1 tsp salt

15ml/1 tbsp Chinese seven-spice powder

15ml/1 tbsp mild chilli powder

sunflower oil, for frying

fresh mint leaves, to garnish

steamed rice or noodles and hot chilli sauce, to serve

1 Slice the aubergines into thin discs and pat dry with kitchen paper.

2 Whisk the egg whites in a bowl until light and foamy, but not dry.

3 Combine the cornflour, salt, seven-spice powder and chilli powder and spread evenly on to a large plate.

4 Fill a wok one-third full of oil and heat to 180°C/350°F (or until a cube of bread, dropped into the oil, browns in 15 seconds).

5 Working in batches, dip the aubergine slices in the egg white and then into the spiced flour mixture to coat. Deep-fry for 3–4 minutes, or until crisp and golden.

6 Remove the aubergines with a wire skimmer or slotted spoon and drain well on kitchen paper.

7 Serve the aubergines immediately, garnished with mint leaves and accompany with steamed rice or noodles, and hot chilli sauce for dipping.

Choosing aubergines Choose small, firm aubergines that feel heavy. Select ones with shiny, unblemished skins, and avoid any that feel soft or that are beginning to wrinkle.

Deep-fried bean curd sheets stuffed with spiced vegetables

Bean curd sheets are made from soya milk. The milk is boiled and the skin that forms on the top is then lifted off and dried in sheets. They are available in Asian supermarkets and need to be soaked briefly in water before filling and frying until deliciously crisp and golden.

SERVES 4

30ml/2 tbsp groundnut (peanut) oil

50g/2oz fresh enokitake mushrooms, finely chopped

1 garlic clove, crushed

5ml/1 tsp grated fresh root ginger

4 spring onions (scallions), finely shredded

1 small carrot, cut into thin matchsticks

115g/4oz bamboo shoots, cut into thin matchsticks

15ml/1 tbsp light soy sauce

5ml/1 tsp chilli sauce

5ml/1 tsp sugar

15ml/1 tbsp cornflour (cornstarch)

8 bean curd sheets (approximately 18 x 22cm/7 x 9in each)

sunflower oil, for frying

crisp salad leaves, to serve

1 Heat the groundnut oil in a wok over a high heat and add the chopped mushrooms, garlic, ginger, spring onions, carrot and bamboo shoots. Stir-fry for 2–3 minutes and add the soy sauce, chilli sauce and sugar and toss to mix thoroughly.

2 Remove the vegetables from the heat and place in a sieve to drain the juices. Set aside to cool.

3 In a small bowl, mix the cornflour with 60ml/4 tbsp of cold water to form a smooth paste. Soak the bean curd sheets in a bowl of warm water for 10–15 seconds and then lay them out on a clean worksurface and pat dry with kitchen paper.

4 Brush the edges of one of the bean curd sheets with the cornflour paste and place 30–45ml/2–3 tbsp of the vegetable mixture at one end of the sheet. Fold the edges over towards the centre and roll up tightly to form a neat roll. Repeat with the remaining bean curd sheets and filling.

5 Place the filled rolls on a baking parchment-lined baking sheet or tray, cover and chill for 3–4 hours.

6 To cook, fill a wok one-third full with sunflower oil and heat to 180°C/350°F (or until a cube of bread, dropped into the oil, browns in 15 seconds).

7 Working in batches, deep-fry the rolls for 2–3 minutes, or until crisp and golden. Drain on kitchen paper and serve immediately with crisp salad leaves.

Fragrant rice paper parcels with wilted choi sum

Translucent rice paper makes a wonderfully crisp wrapping for the lightly spiced vegetable and tofu filling. Take care when handling the papers because they are very brittle and can easily be damaged.

SERVES 4

30ml/2 tbsp sunflower oil

90g/3½oz shiitake mushrooms, stalks discarded and finely chopped

30ml/2 tbsp chopped garlic

90g/3½oz water chestnuts, finely chopped

90g/3½oz firm tofu, finely chopped

2 spring onions (scallions), finely chopped

½ red (bell) pepper, seeded and finely chopped

50g/2oz mangetout (snow peas), finely chopped

15ml/1 tbsp light soy sauce

15ml/1 tbsp sweet chilli sauce

45ml/3 tbsp chopped fresh coriander (cilantro)

30ml/2 tbsp chopped fresh mint leaves

90ml/6 tbsp plain (all-purpose) flour

12 medium rice paper wrappers

sunflower oil, for frying

500g/1¼lb choi sum or Chinese greens, roughly sliced or chopped

egg fried rice, to serve

1 Heat the oil in a large wok over a high heat and add the chopped mushrooms. Stir-fry for 3–4 minutes and then add the garlic and stir-fry for a further 1 minute.

2 Add the water chestnuts, tofu, spring onions, red pepper and mangetout to the wok. Stir-fry for 2–3 minutes and then add the soy and sweet chilli sauces. Remove from the heat and stir in the chopped coriander and mint. Leave to cool completely.

3 Place the flour in a bowl and stir in 105ml/7 tbsp of cold water to make a thick, smooth paste.

4 Fill a large bowl with warm water and dip a rice paper wrapper in it for a few minutes until softened. Remove and drain on a dishtowel.

5 Divide the filling into 12 portions and spoon one portion on to the softened rice wrapper. Fold in each side and roll up tightly. Seal the ends with a little of the flour paste. Repeat with the remaining wrappers and filling.

6 Fill a wok one-third full with the oil and heat to 180°C/350°F (or until a cube of bread, dropped into the oil, browns in 15 seconds). Working in batches of 2–3, deep-fry the parcels for 3 minutes until crisp and lightly browned. Drain well on kitchen paper and keep warm.

7 Pour off most of the oil, reserving 30ml/2 tbsp. Place over a medium heat and add the choi sum. Stir-fry for 3–4 minutes. Divide among four warmed bowls and top with the parcels. Serve immediately with egg fried rice.

Golden deep-fried eggs with tamarind dressing

Inspired by the classic Thai dish, Son-in-Law Eggs, this tasty salad combines crispy fried eggs with crunchy, refreshing beansprouts and salad leaves, and a deliciously sweet and tangy tamarind dresssing. Serve as an appetizer or light meal.

SERVES 4

6 large (US extra large) eggs

sunflower oil, for frying

75g/3oz/scant ½ cup palm sugar

90ml/6 tbsp tamarind juice

75ml/5 tbsp fish sauce

6 shallots, finely sliced

4 garlic cloves, thinly sliced

2 red chillies, seeded and thinly sliced

115g/4oz mixed salad leaves

a small handful of coriander (cilantro) leaves

25g/1oz beansprouts

1 Place the eggs in a pan and cover with cold water. Bring to the boil and cook for 4 minutes. Drain and rinse in cold water. Shell and set aside.

2 Fill a wok, one-third full of oil and heat to 170°C/340°C (or until a cube of bread, dropped into the oil, browns in 20 seconds).

3 Using a slotted spoon, lower the eggs, one at a time, into the hot oil. Deep-fry for 2–3 minutes, or until lightly golden. Remove and drain on kitchen paper. Keep warm.

4 Place the palm sugar, tamarind juice and fish sauce in a clean wok with 30ml/2 tbsp of water and bring to the boil, stirring until the sugar dissolves. Reduce the heat, then simmer gently for 3–4 minutes. Transfer the mixture to a bowl and set aside.

5 Wipe out the wok and add 30ml/ 2 tbsp oil. When hot, fry the shallots, garlic and chillies until they are all lightly browned.

6 In a large bowl, toss together the mixed salad leaves, coriander leaves and beansprouts with the tamarind mixture. Divide this among four plates. Cut the fried eggs in half and and divide among the prepared plates. Sprinkle over the shallot mixture and serve immediately.

Fiery tuna spring rolls

This modern take on the classic spring roll is substantial enough to serve as a main meal with noodles and stir-fried greens. Thick slices of tuna are spiced with pungent Japanese wasabi paste and cooked to perfection – with a crisp outer shell and delicious pink tuna inside.

SERVES 4

8 pieces of very fresh thick tuna steak (cut into pieces about 12 x 2.5cm/4½ x 1in)

45ml/3 tbsp light soy sauce

30ml/2 tbsp wasabi

16 mangetout (snow peas), trimmed

8 spring roll wrappers

sunflower oil, for frying

soft noodles and stir-fried Asian greens, to serve

soy sauce and sweet chilli sauce, for dipping

1 Place the tuna in a large, non-metallic dish in a single layer. Mix together the soy sauce and the wasabi and spoon evenly over the fish. Cover and marinate for 10–15 minutes.

2 Meanwhile, blanch the mangetout in boiling water for about 1 minute, drain and refresh under cold water. Drain and pat dry with kitchen paper.

3 Place a spring roll wrapper on a clean worksurface and place a piece of tuna on top. Top with 2 blanched mangetout and fold over the sides and roll up. Brush the edges of the wrappers to seal. Repeat with the remaining tuna, mangetout and spring roll wrappers.

4 Fill a large wok one-third full with oil and heat to 180°C/350°F (or until a cube of bread, dropped into the oil, browns in 15 seconds). Working in batches, deep-fry the spring rolls for 1–2 minutes, or until crisp and golden. Drain the rolls on kitchen paper and serve immediately with soft noodles and Asian greens. Accompany with soy sauce and sweet chilli sauce for dipping.

Crisp-fried Japanese panko prawns

Panko are Japanese-style breadcrumbs, which give a fabulously crunchy result when deep-fried. They make the perfect coating for these tender, juicy prawns, which remain unbelievably succulent when cooked. If you can't find Japanese *panko*, use coarse, dried breadcrumbs instead.

SERVES 4

20 large raw tiger or king prawns (jumbo shrimp)

30ml/2 tbsp cornflour (cornstarch)

3 large (US extra large) eggs, lightly beaten

150g/5oz *panko* (Japanese-style breadcrumbs)

sunflower oil, for frying

4 sheets of nori

400g/14oz cooked sushi rice

wasabi, soy sauce, sweet chilli sauce and pickled ginger, to serve

1 Peel and devein the prawns, leaving the tails on. Using a small, sharp knife, cut down the back of each prawn, without cutting all the way through, and gently press the prawns out flat to butterfly them.

2 Place the cornflour, beaten eggs and *panko* in 3 separate bowls. Dip each prawn first in the cornflour mixture, then in the egg and then in the *panko* to coat evenly. Fill a wok one-third full of sunflower oil and heat to 180°C/350°F (or until a cube of bread browns in 15 seconds).

3 Working in batches, deep-fry the prawns for 1 minute, or until lightly golden and crisp. Remove with a slotted spoon and drain on kitchen paper.

4 Carefully cut each nori sheet into a 10cm/4in square. Place each square on a serving plate and divide the sushi rice among them, then spread out the rice using the back of a spoon. Top each serving with 5 deep-fried prawns and serve with wasabi, soy sauce, sweet chilli sauce and pickled ginger.

Crispy Thai noodle salad

Rice noodles puff up and become light and crispy when deep-fried and make a lovely base for this tangy, fragrant salad. Serve as a snack or light meal, and enjoy the heady combination of spicy chillies, fragrant pork and prawns, and crispy noodles.

SERVES 4

sunflower oil, for frying

115g/4oz rice vermicelli

45ml/3 tbsp groundnut (peanut) oil

2 eggs, lightly beaten with 15ml/
1 tbsp water

30ml/2 tbsp palm sugar

30ml/2 tbsp fish sauce

15ml/1 tbsp rice wine vinegar

30ml/2 tbsp tomato ketchup

1 red chilli, thinly sliced

3 garlic cloves, crushed

5ml/1 tsp finely grated fresh
root ginger

200g/7oz minced (ground) pork

400g/14oz cooked peeled tiger
prawns (shrimp)

4 spring onions (scallions),
finely shredded

60ml/4 tbsp chopped coriander
(cilantro) leaves

1 Fill a wok one-third full of sunflower oil and heat to 180°C/350°F (or until a cube of bread, dropped into the oil, browns in 15 seconds). Working in batches, deep-fry the vermicelli, for 10–20 seconds, or until puffed up. Remove from the wok with a slotted spoon and drain on kitchen paper.

2 Carefully discard the oil and wipe out the wok. Heat 15ml/1 tbsp of the groundnut oil in the wok. Add half the egg mixture and swirl the wok to make a thin omelette. Cook gently for 2–3 minutes, until the egg has just set and then carefully transfer to a board.

3 Repeat with a further 15ml/1 tbsp of groundnut oil and the remaining egg mixture. Place the second omelette on top of the first and roll up into a cylinder. Cut the cylinder crosswise to make thin strips, then set aside.

4 Mix together the palm sugar, fish sauce, rice wine vinegar, tomato ketchup, chilli, garlic and ginger. Stir half this mixture into the pork and mix until thoroughly combined.

5 Heat the remaining groundnut oil in the wok. When hot, add the pork mixture and stir-fry for 4–5 minutes until cooked through and lightly browned. Add the prawns and stir-fry for a further 1–2 minutes.

6 Remove the wok from the heat and add the remaining palm sugar mixture, fried vermicelli, spring onions and coriander and toss to combine.

7 Divide the mixture among four warmed plates and top with the shredded omelette. Serve immediately.

Tangy fish salad with fresh herbs and chilli

Flakes of halibut are deep-fried until crispy and make a wonderful topping for this refreshing salad. The combination of crispy, crunchy textures and fragrant, spicy flavours is unbeatable.

SERVES 4

250g/9oz halibut fillet, skinned

sunflower oil, for frying

1 cucumber, seeded and thinly sliced

2 plum tomatoes, seeded and diced

1 red onion, halved and thinly sliced

1 large handful of fresh coriander (cilantro) leaves

1 large handful of fresh mint leaves

30ml/2 tbsp sweet chilli sauce

30ml/2 tbsp fish sauce

juice of 2 limes

15ml/1 tbsp soft light brown sugar

45ml/3 tbsp roasted peanuts, chopped

lime wedges, to serve

1 Place the fish in a wok and cover with cold water. Place over a medium heat and bring to the boil. Reduce the heat and cook gently for 6–8 minutes, or until the fish is cooked.

2 Remove the fish from the wok and pat dry on kitchen paper. Break up into large flakes. Place in a food processor and pulse until the mixture resembles coarse breadcrumbs.

3 Fill a wok one-third full with the oil and heat until 180°C/350°F (or until a cube of bread, dropped into the oil, browns in 15 seconds). Working in batches, deep-fry the fish mixture for 1–2 minutes until lightly browned and crispy. Drain and set aside.

4 Combine the cucumber, tomatoes, red onion and herbs in a bowl. Mix together the sweet chilli sauce, fish sauce, lime juice and sugar and pour this over the salad. Sprinkle over the deep-fried fish and chopped peanuts. Serve immediately with lime wedges.

Deep-fried skate wings with wasabi mayo

Whole skate wings dipped in a tempura batter and deep-fried until crisp and golden look stunning and taste delicious. The creamy, zesty mayonnaise flavoured with soy sauce, fiery wasabi paste and spring onions makes a great accompaniment.

SERVES 4

4 x 250g/9oz skate wings

65g/2½oz/9 tbsp cornflour (cornstarch)

65g/2½oz/9 tbsp plain (all-purpose) flour

5ml/1 tsp salt

5ml/1 tsp Chinese five-spice powder

15ml/1 tbsp sesame seeds

200ml/7fl oz/scant 1 cup ice-cold soda water

sunflower oil, for frying

FOR THE MAYONNAISE

200ml/7fl oz/scant 1 cup mayonnaise

15ml/1 tbsp light soy sauce

finely grated rind and juice of 1 lime

5ml/1 tsp wasabi

15ml/1 tbsp finely chopped spring onion (scallion)

1 Using kitchen scissors, trim away the frill from the edges of the skate wings and discard. Set aside.

2 In a large mixing bowl combine the cornflour, plain flour, salt, five-spice powder and sesame seeds. Gradually pour in the soda water and stir to mix. (It will be quite lumpy.)

3 Fill a large wok one-third full of sunflower oil and heat to 190°C/375°F (or until a cube of bread, dropped into the oil, browns in 10 seconds). One at a time, dip the skate wings in the batter and deep-fry for 4–5 minutes, until cooked through. Drain on kitchen paper. Set aside and keep warm.

4 Meanwhile, mix together all the mayonnaise ingredients and divide among four small bowls. Serve immediately with the skate wings.

Spiced scallops and sugar snap peas on crispy noodle cakes

Tender, juicy scallops and sugar snap peas cooked in spices and served on a bed of deep-fried noodles is a winning combination. It's simple and stylish and makes a great dish for entertaining. You can use prawns in place of the scallops if you prefer.

SERVES 4

45ml/3 tbsp oyster sauce

10ml/2 tsp soy sauce

5ml/1 tsp sesame oil

5ml/1 tsp golden caster (superfine) sugar

30ml/2 tbsp sunflower oil

2 red chillies, finely sliced

4 garlic cloves, finely chopped

10ml/2 tsp finely chopped fresh root ginger

250g/9oz sugar snap peas, trimmed

500g/1¼lb king scallops, cleaned, roes discarded and sliced in half

3 spring onions (scallions), finely shredded

FOR THE NOODLE CAKES

250g/9oz fresh thin egg noodles

10ml/2 tsp sesame oil

120ml/4fl oz/½ cup sunflower oil

1 Cook the noodles in a wok of boiling water for 1 minute, or until tender. Drain well and transfer to a bowl with the sesame oil and 15ml/1 tbsp of the sunflower oil. Spread the noodles out on a large baking sheet and leave to dry in a warm place for 1 hour.

2 To cook the noodles, heat 15ml/ 1 tbsp of the oil in a non-stick wok over a high heat. Divide the noodle mixture into four portions and add one portion to the wok. Using a spatula, flatten it out and shape it into a cake.

3 Reduce the heat slightly and cook the cake for about 5 minutes on each side, or until crisp and golden. Drain on kitchen paper and keep warm while you make the remaining three noodle cakes in the same way.

4 Mix together the oyster sauce, soy sauce, sesame oil and sugar in a small bowl, stirring until the sugar has dissolved completely.

5 Heat a wok over a medium heat and add the sunflower oil. When hot add the chillies, garlic and ginger, and stir-fry for 30 seconds. Add the sugar snap peas and stir-fry for 1–2 minutes.

6 Add the scallops and spring onions to the wok and cook over a high heat for 1 minute. Stir in the oyster sauce mixture and cook for a further 1 minute until warmed through.

7 To serve, place a noodle cake on each of four warmed plates and top each one with the scallop mixture. Serve immediately.

Lemon and sesame chicken

These delicate strips of chicken are at their best if you have time to leave them to marinate overnight so that they can really soak up the flavours. The subtle fragrance of lemon really enhances the rich taste of fried chicken and the nutty sesame seeds.

SERVES 4

4 large chicken breast fillets, skinned and cut into strips

15ml/1 tbsp light soy sauce

15ml/1 tbsp Chinese rice wine

2 garlic cloves, crushed

10ml/2 tsp finely grated fresh root ginger

1 egg, lightly beaten

150g/5oz cornflour (cornstarch)

sunflower oil, for frying

toasted sesame seeds, to sprinkle

rice or noodles, to serve

FOR THE SAUCE

15ml/1 tbsp sunflower oil

2 spring onions (scallions), finely sliced

1 garlic clove, crushed

10ml/2 tsp cornflour (cornstarch)

90ml/6 tbsp chicken stock

10ml/2 tsp finely grated lemon zest

30ml/2 tbsp lemon juice

10ml/2 tsp sugar

2.5ml/½ tsp sesame oil

salt

1 Place the chicken strips in a large, non-metallic bowl. Mix together the light soy sauce, rice wine, garlic and ginger and pour over the chicken. Toss together to combine.

2 Cover the chicken and place in the refrigerator for 8–10 hours, or overnight if time permits.

3 When ready to cook, add the beaten egg to the chicken and mix well, then tip the mixture into a colander to drain off any excess marinade and egg.

4 Place the cornflour in a large plastic bag and add the chicken pieces. Shake it vigorously to thoroughly coat the chicken strips.

5 Fill a wok one-third full of sunflower oil and heat to 180°C/350°F (or until a cube of bread, dropped into the oil, browns in 15 seconds).

6 Deep-fry the chicken, in batches, for 3–4 minutes. Lift out the chicken using a slotted spoon and drain on kitchen paper. Reheat the oil and deep-fry the chicken once more, in batches, for 2–3 minutes. Remove with a slotted spoon and drain on kitchen paper. Pour the oil out and wipe out the wok with kitchen paper.

7 To make the sauce, place the sunflower oil in a wok and heat. Add the spring onions and garlic and stir-fry for 1–2 minutes. Mix together the cornflour, stock, lemon zest, lemon juice, sugar, sesame oil and salt and pour into the wok. Cook over a high heat for 2–3 minutes until thickened. Return the chicken to the sauce, toss lightly and sprinkle over the toasted sesame seeds. Serve with rice or noodles.

Sweet and sour pork

This classic Chinese-style dish with its stunning colours and sweet, sour, piquant sauce and gloriously sticky texture makes a tasty supper dish. Serve with fried rice and steamed Asian greens to create an authentic Chinese meal.

SERVES 4

45ml/3 tbsp light soy sauce

15ml/1 tbsp Chinese rice wine

15ml/1 tbsp sesame oil

5ml/1 tsp freshly ground black pepper

500g/1¼lb pork loin, cut into 1cm/½in cubes

65g/2½oz/9 tbsp cornflour (cornstarch)

65g/2½oz/9 tbsp plain (all-purpose) flour

5ml/1 tsp bicarbonate of soda (baking soda)

sunflower oil, for frying

10ml/2 tsp finely grated garlic

5ml/1 tsp finely grated fresh root ginger

60ml/4 tbsp tomato sauce

30ml/2 tbsp caster (superfine) sugar

15ml/1 tbsp rice vinegar

15ml/1 tbsp cornflour (cornstarch) blended with 120ml/4fl oz/ ½ cup water

4 spring onions (scallions), shredded

1 carrot, shredded

1 red (bell) pepper, shredded

egg fried rice or noodles, to serve

salt

1 In a large mixing bowl, combine 15ml/1 tbsp of the soy sauce with the rice wine, sesame oil and pepper. Add the pork and toss to mix. Cover and chill for 3–4 hours.

2 Combine the cornflour, plain flour and bicarbonate of soda in a bowl. Add a pinch of salt and mix in 150ml/¼ pint/ ⅔ cup cold water to make a thick batter. Add the pork to the batter and mix well with your hands to coat evenly.

3 Fill a wok one-third full with the sunflower oil and heat to 180°C/350°F (or until a cube of bread browns in 15 seconds). Separate the pork cubes and deep-fry them, in batches, for 1–2 minutes, or until golden. Remove and drain on kitchen paper.

4 Place a clean wok over a medium heat. Mix together the garlic, ginger, tomato sauce, sugar, the remaining soy sauce, rice vinegar and cornflour mixture. Add to the wok and stir for 2–3 minutes, until thickened. Add the spring onions, carrot and red pepper, stir and remove from the heat.

5 Reheat the deep frying oil in the wok to 180°C/350°F and then re-fry the pork pieces in batches for 1–2 minutes, until golden and crisp. Drain and add to the sauce and toss to mix well. Serve with egg -fried rice or noodles.

Sweet and sumptuous

spiced syrups, steamed custards, sticky desserts and sugary snacks

Woks aren't just for cooking savoury dishes – they can be great for making desserts as well. The only important thing to remember is that when cooking acidic ingredients such as fruit, always use a non-stick or stainless steel wok. From poached fruit in a fragrant syrup and Chinese-style toffee apples to sweet and spicy rice fritters and caramelized fruit tossed in a sugary glaze, there are desserts and sweet treats for every occasion. Try delicate steamed custards that melt in the mouth for a party, or indulge in piping hot steamed puddings scented with ginger when you're looking for the ultimate comfort food. Crispy wontons filled with mango are great any time, and pancakes drizzled with honey are good morning, noon or night!

Crispy mango wontons
with raspberry drizzle sauce

These crisp, golden parcels filled with meltingly sweet, hot mango are perfect for a casual supper or a sophisiticated dinner. The sweet raspberry sauce looks stunning drizzled over the wontons and tastes even better. Serve any extra sauce in a bowl so guests can add more.

SERVES 4

2 firm, ripe mangoes

24 fresh wonton wrappers (approximately 7.5cm/3in square)

oil, for frying

icing sugar, to dust

FOR THE SAUCE

400g/14oz/3½ cups raspberries

45ml/3 tbsp icing (confectioners') sugar

a squeeze of lemon juice

1 First make the sauce. Place the raspberries and icing sugar in a food processor and blend until smooth. Press the raspberry purée through a sieve (strainer) to remove the seeds, then stir a squeeze of lemon juice into the sauce. Cover and place in the refrigerator until ready to serve.

2 Peel the mango, then carefully slice the flesh away from one side of the flat stone (pit). Repeat on the second side, then trim off any remaining flesh from around the stone. Cut the mango flesh into 1cm/½in dice.

3 Lay 12 wonton wrappers on a clean work surface and place 10ml/2 tsp of the chopped mango in the centre of each one. Brush the edges with water and top with the remaining wonton wrappers. Press the edges to seal.

4 Heat the oil in a wok to 180°C/350°F (or until a cube of bread, dropped into the oil, browns in 15 seconds). Deep-fry the wontons, 2–3 at a time, for about 2 minutes, or until crisp and golden. Remove from the oil using a slotted spoon and drain on kitchen paper. Dust the wontons with icing sugar and serve on individual plates drizzled with the raspberry sauce.

Chinese-style toffee apples

This classic dessert will make a great end to any meal. Wedges of crisp apple are encased in a light batter, then dipped in crispy caramel to make a sweet, sticky dessert that is guaranteed to get stuck in your teeth! You can use baby bananas in place of the apples if you prefer.

SERVES 4

115g/4oz/1 cup plain
(all-purpose) flour

10ml/2 tsp baking powder

60ml/4 tbsp cornflour (cornstarch)

4 firm apples

sunflower oil, for frying

200g/7oz/1 cup caster
(superfine) sugar

1 In a large mixing bowl, combine the flour, baking powder, cornflour and 175ml/6fl oz/¾ cup water. Stir to make a smooth batter and set aside.

2 Peel and core the apples, then cut each one into 8 thick wedges.

3 Fill a wok one-third full of oil and heat to 180°C/350°F (or until a cube of bread, dropped into the oil browns in 15 seconds).

4 Working quickly, in batches, dip the apple wedges in the batter, drain off any excess and deep-fry for about 2 minutes, or until golden brown. Remove with a slotted spoon and drain on kitchen paper.

5 Reheat the oil to 180°C/350°F and re-fry the apple wedges again for 2 minutes. Drain well on kitchen paper and set aside.

6 Very carefully, pour off all but 30ml/ 2 tbsp of the oil from the wok and stir in the sugar. Heat gently until the sugar melts and starts to caramelize. When the mixture is light brown, add a few pieces of apple at a time and toss to coat evenly. Just before serving, fill a large bowl with ice cubes and chilled water. Plunge the coated apple pieces briefly into the iced water to harden the caramel, then remove with a slotted spoon and serve immediately.

Sesame and banana fritters

Deep-fried bananas are popular all over South-east Asia, and this version coated in coconut and sesame seeds is particularly good. Small apple bananas, which have a lovely sweet, luscious flavour, are used here, but if you can't find them, you can use larger bananas instead – just cut into bitesize pieces.

SERVES 4

50g/2oz desiccated (dry unsweetened shredded) coconut

50g/2oz/¼ cup golden caster (superfine) sugar

5ml/1 tsp ground cinnamon

2.5ml/½ tsp baking powder

115g/4oz/1 cup rice flour

30ml/2 tbsp sesame seeds

600ml/1 pint/2½ cups coconut milk

6 baby or apple bananas

sunflower oil, for frying

icing (confectioners') sugar, to dust

vanilla ice cream, to serve

1 Place the coconut, golden caster sugar, cinnamon, baking powder, rice flour, sesame seeds and coconut milk in a large mixing bowl. Whisk thoroughly to form a smooth batter.

2 Cover the bowl with clear film (plastic wrap) and place in the refrigerator to rest for 30 minutes–1 hour.

3 When ready to cook, peel the bananas and carefully slice the flesh in half lengthways.

4 Fill a wok one-third full of sunflower oil and heat to 180°C/350°F (or until a cube of bread, dropped into the oil, browns in 15 seconds). Working in batches, dip the halved bananas into the batter, drain off any excess and gently lower into the oil. Deep-fry for 3–4 minutes, or until golden.

5 Remove the bananas from the wok using a slotted spoon and drain well on kitchen paper. Serve hot or warm, dusted with icing sugar, with scoops of vanilla ice cream.

Sweet and spicy rice fritters

These delicious little golden balls of rice are scented with sweet, warm spices and will fill the kitchen with wonderful aromas while you're cooking. To enjoy them at their best, serve piping hot, as soon as you've dusted them with sugar. They are great at any time of day – as a mid-morning or late afternoon snack, a simple dessert, or even as a late night treat after a night out.

SERVES 4

175g/6oz cooked basmati rice

2 eggs, lightly beaten

60ml/4 tbsp caster (superfine) sugar

a pinch of nutmeg

2.5ml/½ tsp ground cinnamon

a pinch of ground cloves

10ml/2 tsp vanilla essence (extract)

50g/2oz/½ cup plain
(all-purpose) flour

10ml/2 tsp baking powder

a pinch of salt

25g/1oz desiccated (dry unsweetened
shredded) coconut

sunflower oil, for frying

icing (confectioners') sugar,
to dust

1 Place the cooked rice, eggs, sugar, nutmeg, cinnamon, cloves and vanilla essence in a large bowl and whisk to combine. Sift in the flour, baking powder and salt and add the coconut. Mix well until thoroughly combined.

2 Fill a wok one-third full of the oil and heat to 180°C/350°F (or until a cube of bread, dropped into the oil, browns in 15 seconds).

3 Very gently, drop tablespoonfuls of the mixture into the oil, one at a time, and fry for 2–3 minutes, or until golden. Carefully remove the fritters from the wok using a slotted spoon and drain well on kitchen paper.

4 Divide the fritters into four portions, or simply pile them up on a single large platter. Dust them with icing sugar and serve immediately.

Gluten-free Unlike many cakes and cookies, these little fritters are gluten-free so make a perfect sweet snack for anyone with a gluten intolerance.

Zesty orange and date buttermilk pancakes

Serve these sweet, sticky, golden pancakes for breakfast, brunch or dessert. They're bursting with the flavour of zesty orange and sweet juicy dates and are utterly moreish. Medjool dates have an intensely sweet flesh and lovely texture and will give the best results.

SERVES 4

150g/5oz/1 ¼ self raising (self-rising) flour

2.5ml/½ tsp baking powder

a pinch of salt

250ml/8fl oz/1 cup buttermilk

3 eggs

15ml/1 tbsp caster (superfine) sugar

200g/7oz/1 ¼ cup Medjool dates, stoned

finely grated zest and juice from 1 small orange

50g/2oz/¼ cup unsalted butter, melted

sunflower oil, for greasing

clear honey, to drizzle

natural (plain) yogurt, to serve

1 Sift the flour and baking soda into a large bowl with a pinch of salt. Whisk in the buttermilk, eggs, sugar, dates, orange zest and juice and melted butter to form a thick batter. Leave to stand for 15 minutes

2 Brush a non-stick wok with a little oil and heat over a medium heat. When hot, pour a small ladleful of the mixture into the wok. Cook for 2–3 minutes, or until just set and golden brown on the underside, then flip over and cook on the second side for 35–45 seconds. Transfer to a plate and keep warm while you cook the remaining batter in the same way. (You should make about 16 pancakes in total.)

3 To serve, divide the pancakes among four warmed plates, piling them up in a stack. Drizzle honey over each stack and top with a dollop of yogurt.

Vanilla, honey and saffron pears

These sweet juicy pears poached in a vanilla-, saffron- and lime-infused honey syrup make a truly elegant dessert. For a low-fat version you can eat them on their own, but for a really luxurious, indulgent treat, serve with cream or ice cream.

SERVES 4

150g/5oz/¾ cup caster (superfine) sugar

105ml/7 tbsp clear honey

5ml/1 tsp finely grated lime rind

a large pinch of saffron

2 vanilla pods (beans)

4 large, firm ripe dessert pears

single (light) cream or ice cream, to serve

1 Place the caster sugar and honey in a medium, non-stick wok, then add the lime rind and the saffron. Using a small, sharp knife, split the vanilla pods in half and scrape the seeds into the wok, then add the vanilla pods as well.

2 Pour 500ml/17fl oz/scant 2¼ cups water into the wok and bring the mixture to the boil. Reduce the heat to low and simmer, stirring occasionally, while you prepare the pears.

3 Peel the pears, then add to the wok and gently turn in the syrup to coat evenly. Cover the wok and simmer gently for 12–15 minutes, turning the pears halfway through cooking, until they are just tender.

4 Lift the pears from the syrup using a slotted spoon and transfer to four serving bowls. Set aside.

5 Bring the syrup back to the boil and cook gently for about 10 minutes, or until reduced and thickened. Spoon the syrup over the pears and serve either warm or chilled with single cream or ice cream.

Perfect flavours For the best result, use firm, ripe dessert pears such as comice or conference. You can also try using different flavourings in the syrup. Use 10ml/2 tsp chopped fresh root ginger and 1 or 2 star anise in place of the saffron and vanilla, or 1 cinnamon stick, 3 cloves and 105ml/7tbsp maple syrup in place of the spices and honey.

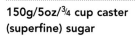

Caramelized pineapple in lemon grass syrup

This stunning dessert, garnished with jewel-like pomegranate seeds is superb for entertaining. The tangy, zesty flavours of lemon grass and mint bring out the exquisite sweetness of the pineapple to create a truly luscious combination. A spoonful of pure, creamy crème fraîche contrasts beautifully with the golden fruit.

SERVES 4

30ml/2 tbsp very finely chopped lemon grass, and 2 lemon grass stalks, halved lengthways

350g/12oz/1¾ cups caster (superfine) sugar

10ml/2 tsp chopped fresh mint leaves

2 small, ripe pineapples (approximately 600g/1lb 5oz each)

15ml/1 tbsp sunflower oil

60ml/4 tbsp pomegranate seeds

crème fraîche, to serve

1 Place all of the lemon grass, 250g/9oz of the sugar and the mint leaves in a non-stick wok. Pour over 150ml/¼ pint/⅔ cup of water and place over a medium heat and bring to the boil.

2 Reduce the heat under the wok and simmer the mixture for 10–15 minutes, until thickened. Strain into a glass bowl, reserving the halved lemon grass stalks, then set aside.

3 Using a sharp knife, peel and core the pineapples and cut into 1cm/½in-thick slices, then sprinkle the slices with the remaining sugar.

4 Brush a large non-stick wok with the oil and place over a medium heat. Working in batches, cook the sugared pineapple slices for 4–5 minutes, on each side, until lightly caramelised.

5 Transfer the pineapple slices to a flat serving dish and scatter over the pomegranate seeds.

6 Pour the lemon grass syrup over the fruit and garnish with the reserved stalks. Serve with crème fraîche.

Removing pomegranate seeds Halve the fruit and hold it over a bowl, cut side down. Tap all over with a wooden spoon and the seeds should drop out.

Caramelized plums
with sticky coconut rice

Red, juicy plums are quickly seared in a wok with sugar to make a rich caramel coating, then served with sticky coconut-flavoured rice for a satisfying dessert. The glutinous rice is available from Asian stores, but remember that you have to soak it overnight before you start.

SERVES 4

6 or 8 firm, ripe plums

90g/3½oz/½ cup caster (superfine) sugar

FOR THE RICE

115g/4oz sticky glutinous rice

150ml/¼ pint/⅔ cup coconut cream

45ml/3 tbsp caster (superfine) sugar

a pinch of salt

1 First prepare the rice. Rinse it in several changes of water, then leave to soak overnight in a bowl of cold water.

2 Line a large bamboo steamer with muslin (cheesecloth). Drain the rice and spread out evenly on the muslin.

3 Cover the rice and steam over simmering water for 25–30 minutes, until the rice is tender. (Check the water level and add more if necessary.)

4 Transfer the steamed rice to a wide bowl and set aside for a moment.

5 Combine the coconut cream with the sugar and salt and pour into to a clean wok. Heat gently and bring to a boil, then remove from the heat and pour over the rice. Stir to mix well.

6 Using a sharp knife, cut the plums in half and remove their stones (pits). Sprinkle the sugar over the cut sides.

7 Heat a non-stick wok over a medium-high flame. Working in batches, place the plums in the wok, cut side down, and cook for 1–2 minutes, or until the sugar caramelizes. (You might have to wipe out the wok with kitchen paper in between batches.)

8 Mould the rice into rounds and place on warmed plates, then spoon over the caramelized plums. Alternatively, simply spoon the rice into four warmed bowls and top with the plums.

Sweet rice vermicelli

The combination of sweetened rice vermicelli, dried fruit, nuts and spices may sound a little unusual, but it makes a deliciously sticky, moist, aromatic dessert that tastes absolutely divine drizzled with cream or served with big scoops of ice cream.

SERVES 4

60g/2½oz/5 tbsp unsalted (sweet) butter

60ml/4 tbsp vegetable oil

185g/6½oz thin rice vermicelli, broken into 3cm/1¼in lengths

1.5ml/¼ tsp ground allspice

30ml/2 tbsp roasted cashew nuts

15ml/1 tbsp chopped almonds

30ml/2 tbsp sultanas (golden raisins)

50g/2oz/⅓ cup ready-to-eat dried apricots, roughly chopped

90g/3½oz/½ cup caster (superfine) sugar

175ml/6fl oz/¾ cup warm water

15ml/1 tbsp rose water

pistachio nuts, to garnish

single (light) cream or ice cream, to serve (optional)

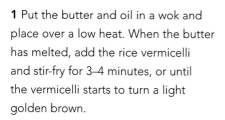

1 Put the butter and oil in a wok and place over a low heat. When the butter has melted, add the rice vermicelli and stir-fry for 3–4 minutes, or until the vermicelli starts to turn a light golden brown.

2 Add the allspice, cashew nuts, almonds, sultanas and apricots to the wok and stir-fry for 1–2 minutes.

3 Sprinkle the sugar over the vermicelli mixture and stir to combine, then add the warm water. Cover and bring to the boil. Reduce the heat and simmer very gently for 8–10 minutes until all the liquid has been absorbed and the vermicelli is tender.

4 Stir the rose water into the vermicelli mixture until well mixed, then ladle into individual warmed bowls, scatter over the pistachio nuts and serve with single cream or ice cream if liked.

Rich spiced carrot and raisin halwa

This is another unusual dessert that tastes absolutely delicious. Halwa is a classic Indian sweet, and there are many variations. Here grated carrots are cooked in milk with ghee, sugar, spices and raisins until meltingly tender and sweet. You will only need a small bowl because it is very rich.

SERVES 4

90g/3½oz ghee

300g/11oz carrots, coarsely grated

250ml/8fl oz/1 cup milk

150g/5oz/¾ cup golden caster (superfine) sugar

5–6 lightly crushed cardamom pods

1 clove

1 cinnamon stick

50g/2oz/scant ½ cup raisins

1 Place a wok over a low heat and add half the ghee. When the ghee has melted, add the grated carrot and stir-fry for 6–8 minutes.

2 Pour the milk into the wok and bring to the boil, reduce the heat to low and simmer gently for 10–12 minutes.

3 Stir the remaining ghee into the carrot mixture, then stir in the sugar, crushed cardamom pods, clove, cinnamon stick and raisins.

4 Gently simmer the carrot mixture for 6–7 minutes, stirring occasionally, until thickened and glossy. Serve immediately in small serving bowls.

Ghee This clarified butter is widely used in Indian cooking. It is an essential ingredient in halwa and is available in cans from Asian stores.

Steamed coconut and mandarin custards with nut praline

These scented custards with a fabulous melt-in-the-mouth texture are best served warm. However, they are also delicious served chilled, making them perfect for hassle-free entertaining. You can make the praline a few days in advance and simply store in an airtight container.

SERVES 4

200ml/7fl oz/scant 1 cup coconut cream

200ml/7fl oz/scant 1 cup double (heavy) cream

2.5ml/¹⁄₂ tsp finely ground star anise

75ml/5 tbsp golden caster (superfine) sugar

15ml/1 tbsp very finely grated mandarin or orange rind

4 egg yolks

FOR THE PRALINE

175g/6oz/scant 1 cup caster (superfine) sugar

50g/2oz/¹⁄₂ cup roughly chopped mixed nuts (cashews, almonds and peanuts)

1 Make the praline. Place the sugar in a non-stick wok with 15–30ml/1–2 tbsp water. Cook over a medium heat for 6–8 minutes, until the sugar dissolves and the mixtures turns light gold.

2 Remove the syrup from the heat and pour on to a baking sheet lined with baking parchment. Spread out using the back of a spoon, then sprinkle the chopped nuts evenly over the top and leave to harden.

3 Meanwhile place the coconut cream, double cream, star anise, sugar, mandarin or orange rind and egg yolks in a large bowl. Whisk to combine and pour the mixture into 4 lightly greased ramekins or small, heatproof bowls.

4 Place the ramekins or cups in a large steamer, cover and place in a wok and steam over gently simmering water for 12–15 minutes, or until the custards are just set.

5 Carefully lift the custards from the steamer and leave to cool slightly for about 10 minutes.

6 To serve, break up the praline into rough pieces and serve on top of, or alongside, the custards.

Lemon, ginger and pistachio steamed puddings

These decadently moist little desserts flavoured with lemon and ginger and served with a luscious cardamom-spiced syrup will definitely become a firm family favourite. They're deliciously moreish and make a particularly good winter dessert.

SERVES 4

150g/5oz/10 tbsp butter

150g/5oz/¾ cup golden caster (superfine) sugar

10ml/2 tsp ground ginger

finely grated rind of 2 lemons

2 eggs

150g/5oz/1¼ cups self-raising (self-rising) flour

a pinch of salt

115g/4oz/1 cup finely chopped pistachio nuts

shredded lemon rind, pistachio nuts and chopped preserved stem ginger, to garnish

FOR THE SYRUP

150g/5oz/¾ cup golden caster (superfine) sugar

1.5ml/¼ tsp crushed cardamom seeds

5ml/1 tsp ground ginger

10ml/2 tsp finely grated lemon rind and juice of 2 lemons

5ml/1 tsp arrowroot powder

1 Make the syrup. Place the sugar, cardamom seeds and ginger in a non-stick wok and pour in 150ml/¼ pint/⅔ cup water. Heat gently until the sugar has dissolved completely, then add the lemon rind and juice. Bring to the boil and cook for 3–4 minutes.

2 Mix the arrowroot with 30ml/2 tbsp cold water and whisk into the syrup. Simmer gently for 2 minutes, or until the syrup has thickened slightly. Transfer to a bowl and set aside.

3 Grease 4 x 200ml/7fl oz/scant 1 cup heatproof bowls and set aside.

4 In a clean bowl whisk together the butter and sugar until pale and fluffy. Add the ginger and beat in the eggs, one at a time. Sift in the flour and salt and add the chopped nuts, mixing thoroughly to combine.

5 Spoon 20ml/4 tsp of the syrup into the base of each greased bowl (reserving the remaining syrup) and swirl to coat the sides. Spoon in the pudding mixture and level the tops. Cover tightly with greaseproof (waxed) paper or foil and secure with string.

6 Place the puddings in a bamboo steamer. Pour about 5cm/2in boiling water into a wok and place the steamer over it. Cover and steam for 1 hour and 15 minutes (replenishing the water when necessary), until the puddings have risen and are firm to the touch.

7 Reheat the remaining syrup, then carefully unmould the puddings on to individual plates and spoon over the syrup. Garnish with the lemon rind, pistachio nuts and preserved stem ginger and serve immediately.

Index